THE ART OF FALLING
FREESTYLE SLALOM SKATING

THE ART OF FALLING

FREESTYLE SLALOM SKATING

NAOMI GRIGG

The Art of Falling: Freestyle Slalom Skating

Copyright 2014 by Naomi Grigg

ISBN-13: 978-0692227374 (Patson Media)
ISBN-10: 0692227377

1 June 2014

Foreword by Sebastien Laffargue
Cover design by Ohsik Park
Illustrations by Joe Walker
Photography by Natalie Ujuk
Cover photograph by Keanoush Da Rosa

Published by Patson Media LLC
San Francisco, California
info@patson.com

CONTENTS

Foreword 1
Publisher's Note 3
Introduction 5

BENEFITS OF FREESTYLE TO OTHER TYPES OF SKATING   7

Edge Control 9
Weight Distribution 9
Speed Skating 10
Low Speed Learning 10
Physiotherapy Exercises for Skating 10
Stopping and Turning 11
Agility 11

EQUIPMENT   13

The Boot 15
    What you need from a boot
    Types of boot
    How to do them up
    The Frame

Wheels 18
    Size
    Hardness
    Profile
    Brand/compound
    When to replace your wheels
    Rotation
    Rockering

Bearings 22
    ABEC Rating
    Ceramic Bearings
    Cleaning your bearings
    Common Misconceptions

Heel Brakes 24

Customisation 24
Protection 25
    Level of risk
    How much risk are you happy with?
    Awareness of the consequences of your choices
    Types of protection available

GETTING READY   29

Choosing and Setting up your Area 31
    Location
    Cones
    The Cone Line(s)
    Measuring Instruments

Body Conditioning 33
    Flexibility and Stretching
    Strength and Cardiovascular Fitness

Lessons 33
    What an instructor can give you
    Are lessons for you?
    Qualifications
    How to get the most out of instruction

Learning Tricks From Videos 37

FOUNDATION TRICKS   39

Foundation Tricks 41
Crisscross 44
Snake 46
Basketweave 48
1-Foot 50
Nelson 52
Back Cross 54
Backward Snake 56
Back 1-Foot 58
Back Nelson 60
Mega 62
Sun 64

PIVOTS: THE PARTICLE THEORY OF SKATING — 67

Introducing the 24 Pivots — 69

Troubleshooting — 70

The Edge of the Satellite foot — 73

The Most Valuable Pivots — 74
- *The Forward Uncrossed Heel Pivot*
- *The Backward Uncrossed Toe Pivot*
- *The Backward Crossed-Behind Toe Pivot ('Volte')*

Using Pivots to solve problems and learn tricks — 76
- *Breaking tricks down into pivots*

How to Use the Pivots — 77
- *Sun*
- *Crazy*
- *Mabrouk*
- *Screw*
- *Backward heel wheeling*

STYLE AND FLOW — 81

What is Style? — 83

Good Style = Technical Achievement — 83

Elements — 84
- *Posture/Form*
- *Fluidity and Smoothness*
- *Power/Energy*
- *Whipping*

SKILLS AND DRILLS — 97

Skill: One-foot balance and control — 99
- *Drill 1: Skating on one foot*
- *Drill 2: 3-turns*

Skill: Edge control — 101
- *Drill 1: Alternating between edges during toe and heel rolls*
- *Drill 2: Pivots*

Skill: Rotary motion — 102
- *Drill: Pivots*

Skill: Falling 103
    Drill 1: The Gingerbread Man.
    Drill 2: Toppling from pivot to pivot.

Skill: Spotting 105
    Drill: Learning to spot

PRACTISE PRACTISE PRACTISE   107

Practice Exercises 110
    Slow motion
    Visualisation
    Knee-bend exercise
    Technique intervals
    Off Cones Freestyle
    3 times per move

Organising Practice 116

Monthly Projects and Themes 118

Getting Frustrated? 119

PREPARING FOR COMPETITIONS   121

Types of competition 123

Classic Competitions 125
    Judging

Battle Competitions 127
    Judging

Preparing for a Classic Competition 130
    Before the comp
    Finalising the combo
    Perfecting the combo

Preparing for a Battle 137
    Before the comp
    Improvising for Battle
    Last Trick

Tactics 139

The Day of The Competition 140

The Results 142

About the Author 145

Acknowledgements 147

Author's Note 149

Foreword

by Sebastien Laffargue

For as long as I have known Naomi she has always been passionate about how beautiful skating should be. When I met her, she was just starting to try on cones the dancing moves that she had been practising for years as a dance skater.

She did it well, showing people around her that freestyle slalom was not only crossing your legs and going fast through a cone line. She opened many more possibilities, giving real meaning to the word 'freestyle'.

Her flow on the cones became a mix between classic slalom tricks, break dance and roller dance. She then extended her range of original moves by adding different elements, influenced by what she had seen and learned from her numerous trips around the world. To the precision and variety of the European way of doing the tricks, she mixed the craziness and elegance of the Asian style.

All of those experiences around the world made her freestyle unique and so recognisable from the hundreds of other styles of skating.

Besides her ability for skating, Naomi has a real ability to teach people. She is able to make them easily understand how to do a complicated move, by always giving the right advice on how the legs should be, as well as the arms and other parts of the body.

Naomi's patience, no doubt acquired by teaching physics to children in high school, and her sense of analysis are strong qualities that she uses to help her students to skate as they want.

Naomi's motto is 'There is no reason to perform a difficult trick if it doesn't look good when you do it!' She spread this word all around the world, from USA to Australia, the UK, Hong-Kong and Singapore, and encouraged many skaters to follow the belief that skating that looks good usually looks good because of good technique. Everyone who attends Naomi's class keeps this philosophy in mind for everything they will learn in their skating future.

Naomi dedicates herself to skating. She is able to do almost everything on skates, trying all the disciplines she has found on her way. I can remember her wearing the outfit of an aggressive rider, as well as the one of a speed skater, and even that of a roller derby player! I am also a great fan of versatility and I have always believed that you can teach a particular sport of inline skating better if you can also take different techniques here and there from other inline sports. Trying to understand all disciplines makes you more open and more able to adapt your skills to find a way to teach everybody in a different way; to be able to teach someone any move, taking into account his or her particular history, their experience or lack of experience, and of course their own way of moving the body.

Naomi Grigg is not only a great skater, and a great teacher, she has also been involved in the organisation of many events. Most of the time she is the motor that encourages a whole team around her to run a project from the beginning until the end, not only being very concerned about the final presentation of the event, but also how the participants and audience will enjoy it. During events, she has also spent a lot of time behind the judges' table, evaluating performances, giving marks, and complaining to herself when the skaters don't look good when they try to perform a non-stylish difficult trick!

Being an international judge in freestyle competitions all around the world completes Naomi's background, and makes her an expert in analysing and comparing the performance of the world's best skaters. Thanks to her expertise she is able to help skaters, from the early beginner to the future champion, to achieve their own goals in freestyle skating.

Without any doubt, I can say that Naomi has become THE freestyle skater's makeover specialist! Meet her, listen to her, read her words, and you will skate better, and always with style!

Publisher's Note

Smoothness and Fluidity! Smoothness and Fluidity! Those words ring out to me as the central memory from the first time I met Naomi Grigg, when I participated in her freestyle skating workshop in San Francisco a few years back.

I remember being struck by those words, and by the audacity of this young woman, so possessed by the desire to spill her knowledge and enthusiasm onto others, presuming to tell a novice skater like me that the key to scoring well in freestyle competitions was to move beyond technical skills and to perform the tricks with smoothness and fluidity.

But that's Naomi. With professional-level skills and knowledge, and a résumé full of awards and accomplishments to prove it, she spends a great deal of time and effort teaching and encouraging others. And she has this infectious belief that anyone can learn, anyone can improve, given the right bits of information.

I knew I had found something special that day as Naomi went on and on, not only about smoothness and fluidity, but also about a host of other fine points on how to get your body to make your skates go around those little cones in a particular way.

A few years later, as a slightly more accomplished skater, I stumbled across the manuscript to this book, which Naomi had posted online. Reading it, I felt as if I had been transported back to Naomi's workshop, hearing her talk about various aspects of freestyle slalom. But this time I didn't have to absorb it all at once, because it was all there on the page.

I felt in my gut that this was a valuable work that deserved a wider audience.

If you're an experienced freestyle skater, you'll find this an invaluable reference which will reward you each time you open it. If you're more of a beginner skater, as I was, or if you're just interested in learning what freestyle is all about, this book is an invitation to a world of fun and enjoyment.

I'm very pleased to have played a role in making this book available to skaters everywhere. I hope you will read it with interest, and then get out on your skates and just skate!

David Harrison

Introduction

This book is for skaters who want to transform their skating.

Whether you are just getting started in freestyle slalom or are an experienced slalomer, or even a skater from another discipline looking to improve your core skills, the lessons found here will help you pick up tricks faster, improve the quality of your skating and troubleshoot problems. For those who want to compete, there is a chapter covering all the details of that process. The information here is written with inline skaters in mind, but it also applies to quad skaters.

Getting started in freestyle slalom can be intimidating. How on earth do you make your feet weave seemingly impossible patterns? This book will take you through all the basics, including advice on what skates to get and how to set them up, tutorials for a full menu of beginning moves, tips and drills for developing skills and style, and recommendations for continued growth as a slalom skater.

My aim is to make this learning process much faster and easier for you than it was for me. In my youth I would see someone do a trick once and then attempt to copy them, practising that move for weeks on end, improving gradually through mindless repetition. It took me six years to achieve a level of skating that I now see many skaters attain in a single year. Techniques I have developed in my years of studying and teaching can enable students to speed the learning process considerably and make it more fulfilling through intelligent practice. Mastery of the basics is key to this.

The world of freestyle slalom is overflowing with tricks to learn, and newly invented moves are coming out all the time. It is easy to become so caught up in learning the hottest new trick that you neglect the problems at the heart of your skating. You may be able to awkwardly execute that hot new trick, but without a solid foundation of basic skills, you will never be able to do it with beauty and grace.

Until now there have been very few written resources to provide guidance for those who don't have the advantage of easy access to a skilled slalom instructor. I hope this manual will help to fill that gap, and make slalom skating more accessible, no matter where you live.

BENEFITS OF FREESTYLE TO OTHER TYPES OF SKATING

Edge Control 9

Weight Distribution 9

Speed Skating 10

Low Speed Learning 10

Physiotherapy Exercises for Skating 10

Stopping and Turning 11

Agility 11

BENEFITS OF FREESTYLE TO OTHER TYPES OF SKATING

The key skills used and gained during freestyle slalom are used in every other skating discipline. However, whilst the other skating disciplines utilise the same key skills as we do during freestyle slalom, no other discipline develops these skills as highly during the actual doing of the sport. In other disciplines they are usually worked on and developed separately and then applied to their sport. Freestyle slalom develops these skills during normal execution, making slalom very useful as a cross-training activity for other sports – it is as if slalom itself is skill development for other disciplines.

Typically, skaters don't learn to make their skates do the work or use them properly, but if you can master edging and weight distribution, you can put it into speed skating or any other skating discipline.

Here are some of the many ways that freestyle slalom helps your general skating:

Edge Control

Each skate has two edges: inside and outside. On inline skates, this refers to which side of the wheel is in contact with the ground, and on quad skates it refers to which way the plate is leaning. If you stand normally and your skate is leaning towards the other, you are on your 'inside' edge of that skate, and if your skate is leaning away from the other skate, you are using the 'outside' edge.

Each edge is usually equally important when skating, but the inside edges are the most comfortable and safe places to be. Adventuring onto the outside edges during most types of skating is fraught with the risk of overbalancing and falling over, but in freestyle slalom we develop the use of outside edges without stretching the comfort zone so much.

If you feel anything less than fully confident on your outside edges, then your regular skating has a whole lot to gain from learning the basics of Freestyle Slalom.

Weight Distribution

In all types of skating, it is very important to have the weight on one foot or the other at any single moment. Only during static spins do we have our weight on both feet. It also helps to be able to have control over exactly where in each foot our weight is. For example we prefer to have our weight towards the back of the foot during much of the speed skating stride.

In freestyle slalom we don't talk much about where the weight should be in the foot, and most self-taught slalomers have never thought much about which foot the weight should be. But all skaters will automatically develop a greater ability to balance on one foot and choose where their weight is. It is not usually a consciously learned skill in slalom, it is merely a very convenient side effect that comes from our bodies finding a way of making our feet follow patterns on the floor around cones.

Speed Skating

Speed skating is all about becoming mind blowingly good at one trick. Other than the body conditioning and tactics, speed skaters spend most of their skating time getting an ever more efficient and powerful stride.

Pretty much every speed skater has been fully informed as to what the feet and body should be doing in order to go faster with less effort, so why do we still see skaters on 100mm wheels living on the inside edge and having both feet on the floor at the same time? It is because they lack the skills needed for correct technique.

Freestyle slalom skating offers those skills on a platter.

Low Speed Learning

Freestyle slalom usually involves developing skills at very low speeds. This offers two principle advantages:

- **Lower Risk.** It enables the skater to stretch their comfort zone by experiencing new edges, pressures, and skills at a speed where there is little chance of bodily damage. Once experienced at these lower speeds, a skater is then able to use these new skills at speeds at which they would never have felt comfortable developing them.
- **Muscle Memory.** Lower speeds enable far more accurate editing of muscle memory. If you want to become better or more consistent at any movement, practise it in slow motion. It is hard to practise most things in slow motion and usually shortcuts are taken during the tricky bits. Freestyle slalom doesn't allow any shortcuts because there are cones on the ground, policing your technique.

Physiotherapy Exercises for Skating

Freestyle slalom is the skating equivalent of doing physiotherapy exercises. It enables the isolation of particular muscles and particular skills. Whatever is troubling your normal skating, there is a freestyle slalom technique or trick that will solve it.

Stopping and Turning

Stopping on inline skates is so very 1990s. Turning is the new stopping. Why stop when you can just choose to avoid whatever it was that you were on a collision course with? Why stop when you can just drift around in an aimless circle a few times until your energy runs out? It is often said that having a heel brake on the back of your skates hinders development of much needed skills, and it is absolutely true. Sure there are exceptions, but not many.

Freestyle slalom enables you to develop the skills you need to control and dissipate your speed without wanting or needing a block of rubber stuck to the back of a skate. It helps you to learn parallel turns, hockey stops and countless other techniques that will eliminate the need for a heel brake. What Freestyle slalom doesn't do though, is pay for all those wheels you destroy when you T-stop! Having said that, it will certainly reduce the need for T-stopping.

Agility

Sheppard and Young (2006) defined agility as 'a rapid whole body movement with change of velocity or direction in response to a stimulus.' In skating, this acceleration or 'change in velocity' comes from being able to topple your body in any particular direction without hesitation. You must do so in such a way that there are no mechanical barriers to your immediate movement in the chosen direction.

This means that your skates must flick onto the most advantageous edges, your hips, shoulders, head must align themselves in the most appropriate position, your centre of gravity must start falling in the new direction and this must all happen not only immediately and without hesitation, but it must take place as an involuntary action. No conscious thought should be used. This keeps the conscious part of the mind available to make such decisions as "where is the cyclist going to move" and "is there a car coming around this blind corner". You cannot be agile if your RAM is used up with micromanaging the practicality of moving – it makes you sluggish and awkward.

In freestyle slalom, your body automatically develops the skills to fall in all different directions comfortably and with confidence. I often say that slalom is the art of falling from one foot to the other, whether forward, backward or to the side, and agility requires this to be dialled into your automatic reflex.

EQUIPMENT

The Boot 15
    What you need from a boot
    Types of boot
    How to do them up
    The Frame

Wheels 18
    Size
    Hardness
    Profile
    Brand/compound
    When to replace your wheels
    Rotation
    Rockering

Bearings 22
    ABEC Rating
    Ceramic Bearings
    Cleaning your bearings
    Common Misconceptions

Heel Brakes 24

Customisation 24

Protection 25
    Level of risk
    How much risk are you happy with?
    Awareness of the consequences of your choices
    Types of protection available

EQUIPMENT

Firstly, be aware that you can do freestyle in pretty much any skates - speed skates, quad skates, recreational skates, hockey skates, aggressive skates. (If these are your choices, go with the hockey skates!) This is true of any discipline – you can ride ramps with speed skates, recreational skates, freestyle skates or hockey skates as well as the usual aggressive skates and quad skates. Skates are skates, and all that having a specialised skate does is make what you're doing easier. So, don't procrastinate getting started simply because you don't have the 'right' pair for the job.

However, having the correct pair of skates for the job does make freestyle, and particularly freestyle slalom, much much easier! Even the advancements made each year can increase a competitor's chances of being able to hold an edge or perform a 1-wheeled trick.

The Boot

What you need from a boot

- Foot support
- Cuff/ankle support
- Light weight
- Comfortable long term

Types of boot

There are various types of skate boots on the market. Here they are in reverse order of appropriateness for slalom:

- **Soft boot with liner** – These are usually recreational and 'fitness' skates and I do not recommend them for any type of freestyle. They have very high levels of immediate comfort, they do up tightly and handle rough terrain comfortably. The main downside is the lack of support that the foot receives, enabling the foot to move too much. If the foot is able to move inside the skate, your foot muscles are having to work extra hard, you will have a reduced level of control over your edges and controlling your feet will be less accurate. These boots are not good for anyone, let alone a freestyle skater.
- **Hard boot with liner** – These ones are more like a crossover skate used for freeride. They have high levels of immediate comfort and also the ability to handle impact and rough terrain well. The downside is that the increased

ankle support is restrictive during slalom and the hard boot does not closely hug the foot, resulting in a lack of responsiveness and control when skating. The skate is less able to take instructions from you.

- **Speed style boot, with cuff and removable liner** – These are more specifically developed for slalom. They hold the foot with a very secure grip in a speed style boot, with a liner that moulds over time to fit the foot. Because of this liner, they don't cause the discomfort while breaking-in that you often experience with speed and hockey skates. The downsides of this type of skate are that they have a slightly lower level of comfort when they're fresh out of the box and due to the responsiveness that comes in useful during high level slalom moves, you'll also be more sensitive to the quality of road surface you're on than you would be with a hard boot style skate.
- **Speed style boot with cuff and integrated liner** – These have been specifically developed for slalom. They hold the foot with a strong grip, with no removable liner. Instead of a hard cuff holding the ankle, the main ankle support is similar to a stiff liner which is part of the skate. The upsides are more foot control and ankle flexibility.

How to do them up

Do your skates up properly! Don't remove the laces from a boot which you feel is too hard to tighten, but really is not. Some slalom skates may be rigid at the start and not feel like they need the laces, and given the extra time and effort that laces take to do up, it might not seem worth it. However the boots will usually soften over time, particularly those based on speed boots, and you will be faced with two consequences – you won't be getting the support that you need and is available to you, and the boots will degrade faster.

The Frame

The main considerations when judging a freestyle frame are:
- Stiffness
- Weight
- Length

The stiffer the better. It's hard to imagine a frame actually flexing under your weight, but when you're up on one wheel, that's exactly what happens. You can feel this when you're skating as a kind of sluggish resistance. Also, the more it bends, the more likely it is that some part of it will break.

The lighter the better. This hardly needs an explanation – a lighter skate feels better, and is easier to handle.

Length is a difficult one. It used to be widely accepted that shorter was always better and many of us would find shorter and shorter hockey frames for our custom 'ultimate' freestyle creations. Shorter means better manoeuvrability, and makes it easier to go up onto one wheel, since the toe wheel and heel wheel are closer to the centre of the foot. However longer frames have made a comeback – with space for larger wheels, and toe and heel wheels further out, they offer the ability to get more power into your slalom, make bigger and more beautiful arcs, and allow improvements to 1- and 2-wheeled tricks. Longer frames are now seen as offering greater control during one and two wheeled tricks because the quadriceps are used more than with shorter frames, taking pressure off the calf muscles and making the tricks feel more stable. Larger wheels also offer more stability, along with the added benefit of a smoother ride. Common frame lengths for slalom are 231mm and 243mm, which are the minimum lengths that a frame can be whilst holding four 76mm wheels and four 80mm wheels respectively.

Wheels

Since wheels will usually need changing quite a few times during the lifetime of a pair of skates, which wheels to use is often a subject of much discussion. Here is the lowdown on the top 3 issues:

Size

Size is everything. Skaters will be slightly flexible on almost everything but the size and deciding which size of wheels to get is a very simple decision to make, since you already made the decision when choosing your skate and/or frame. You should use the largest wheels you can possibly fit into the frame. Larger wheels offer greater stability for 1- and 2-wheeled tricks, and a smoother ride. Smaller wheels offer freestyle skaters no advantages at all other than the ability to use a shorter frame length.

For a 243mm or longer frame, this will usually mean 76-80-80-76 setup, whilst a 231mm frame will take a 72-76-76-72 setup.

Hardness

The hardness rating of any wheel is important, but only to a point. You should bear in mind that it's all pretty arbitrary, can vary between batches, and is only an indication of hardness – you should check what other skaters have to say about the hardness of a particular wheel from their own personal experience of the quality that you're actually after. Here are the qualities at stake:

- A frictionless ride – also known as speed. The harder a wheel is, the less it will deform under your weight. Reduced deformation means less energy lost as heat, meaning that you're less likely to grind to a halt whilst rolling with all of your weight on one wheel.

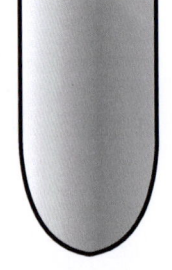

- Better control. The harder a wheel is, and the less it deforms when taking your weight, the rounder the profile will be when rolling. As a result the wheel will be better equipped to respond to the subtle movements in your feet.
- Grip. Not quite such an issue on a dry tarmac, but more of an issue if you're skating on a smooth indoor, or wet surface. A softer wheel will deform more under your weight, and so will have a larger surface area in contact with the ground. Rubbery material is an exception to rules regarding the relationship between

friction and surface area, so the larger the surface area, the more grip you get. Also, the softer the wheel the more able it is to mould to the shape of the ground, and get a better grip.
- Longevity. Generally speaking, the harder the wheel, the longer it will last. It will be more resistant to wear.
- Smoothness of ride. Not quite so important for freestyle skating, but since most of us use our skates for more than just freestyle, it's worth a mention. A harder wheel will keep you intimately acquainted with every rut in the road surface, whereas a softer wheel will keep you more insulated from a bad road surface.

Here is a quick summary of how wheel hardness affects these qualities:
- **Harder**= Faster, less grip, longer lasting, rougher ride, better handling
- **Softer**= Slower, more grip, less long lasting, smoother ride, weaker handling

For freestyle slalom, 83A to 86A is considered ideal, but you can use almost any hardness. I used to use 78A and I was quite happy with them.

Profile

There are 3 main profiles – flat profile, round profile and elliptical profile. Quite simply, elliptical is best for freestyle since it is more sensitive to the actions of the foot.

Brand/compound

This is more important than one might imagine. The manufacturing process and the compound used are two of the most important influences on the performance of a wheel. Paying for a name is often worth it. A good quality wheel will give you a longer lifespan, better rebound (better control and less energy loss during the inevitable deformation), and offer you a better grip without the usual compromises.

My advice is to avoid wheels branded with the names of skate companies and stick to specialised wheel companies. There are exceptions to this rule such as current freestyle brands, which simply put their names onto wheels made by well-respected wheel manufacturers.

Wheels also come in and out of fashion. There are times when everyone wants wheel A, and then there's a move towards wheel B, and wheel A might come back into fashion one day. Try not to get too caught up in what's hot and what's not - I spent years always wearing the cheapest bits of polyurethane that I could find. I can't imagine doing that now that I've become accustomed to the good life of expensive wheels, but all the tricks are still possible on low quality wheels. I know an excellent and competitive slalomer who lives off other people's throwaways, whatever the size or brand.

When to replace your wheels

Really, you can wait until at least one of the wheels has cored, with the hard plastic hub poking through. However, the more worn a wheel is, the worse its properties become and the harder many tricks become, particularly 1- and 2-wheeled tricks.

The deciding factor in the end is usually your budget. You can even wait until at least one wheel is cored on both sides with the remaining rubber hanging off. If this is your philosophy then I recommend replacing them about a week prior to a competition so there is time to wear in the new wheels.

Rotation

I once asked a skating mentor (Iain Francis aka 'Mr Inline') about this, and he just laughed and replied 'ro-what??' I couldn't believe that he didn't rotate his wheels, but now I rarely do either.

For freestyle, the advice offered in the leaflets that come in the box with most skates should be well and truly ignored. All you want to do is ensure equal wear on the inside and outside edges, and for the right and left feet. A perfectly legitimate way of doing this, if you don't care which side of your frame faces outwards, is to switch your frames over. This will switch your right foot wheels onto the left and vice-versa, and convert inside edges to outside edges.

You will also wear down the front faster than the back, or vice-versa, so you might want to consider rotating back to front too if you are willing to deal with the awful adjustment period after you have changed them.

Rockering

Rockering refers to altering the behaviour of your skate by inserting different sized wheels into different positions in your frame, and/or by having only some of your wheels touching the ground at any one time.

Banana Rocker　　　Half Rocker　　　No Rocker

The banana rocker

In freestyle, the term 'rockering' almost always refers to a banana rocker. The increased manoeuvrability and control over the skate that this rocker offers makes it an almost indispensable tool for all types of freestyle skating. I have only found one trick that is easier with a flat rocker (the 'Inverted Barrel Roll', an off-cones trick) – almost all of the others are considerably easier with a banana rocker.

To rocker or not to rocker

The downsides to rockering your skates are the reduction in your top speed when skating in a straight line, and the instability of skating on what can feel like two rocking chairs. There are 4 solutions to these:

- Get over it, get used to it, avoid skate parks (or not) and adjust your technique accordingly. This is the most common option.
- Switch wheels and/or frames depending on what type of skating you're going to be doing. This solution is far too much effort for most of us.
- Use a half banana, where you only rocker the first wheel, leaving the rear 3 wheels flat. This was my solution for a long time, as I also enjoyed jumping over things, riding stairs, and going fast on the streets. It's also a good solution if you feel too unstable to use a full banana rocker for slalom.
- Get your old skates and give them a flat rocker for all other types of skating – this is also good for not wearing out your freestyle wheels when street skating. Most skaters who own freestyle skates don't own them as their first pair, and so have an old pair lurking in a closet somewhere.

Rockering using frames

Frames that come with most freestyle skates are flat and can only be rockered by changing wheel sizes. This is to make the skate more versatile. Older skates had rockerable inserts but these were considered inconvenient and an extra part to cause problems such as wear and tear from not being able to withstand the high forces. There are frames on the market which are pre-rockered, so the axles are higher for the front and back wheels – these are the best solution for skates that are always rockered, because it means you get to have larger wheels for 1- and 2-wheeled tricks. The only problem with these frames is that you can't unrocker them.

Rockering using wheels

If using a flat frame where all the axles are the same height (the most common frame setup), then wheels 2 and 3 should be the largest wheels that you can fit into your frame, and then wheels 1 and 4 should have a diameter 4mm smaller.

If using a hi-lo frame (hockey frames are often hi-lo) where the front two axles are lower than the rear two axles, then achieving a banana rocker is slightly more involved. The simple way to work out what sized wheels to put on is to get the sizes of wheels that would give a flat setup (i.e. all the wheels touching the ground) and then replace the front and back wheels with wheels of 4mm less in diameter.

If using a pre-rockered frame, you just put in all the same sized wheels of course - the largest that the frame can accept.

Bearings

The First Rule of Bearings is, you do not talk about bearings. Every activity has that one topic that makes everyone's eyes roll, and this is the inline skating one. Be warned.

ABEC Rating

ABEC stands for Annular Bearing Engineering Committee, which rates bearings for general industrial use. Bearings are rated ABEC 1, 3, 5, 7 or 9 depending on the precision of the manufacturing process. This precision is very important in many industrial applications where bearings will spin tens of thousands of revolutions per minute (rpm).

While precision is important for bearings, the ABEC rating has no connection to inline skating and doesn't take into account any skate specific qualities that bearings might have.

As a skater, you want a bearing that will last. You want it to cope with impacts, forces from different angles, possibly rain, and you want it to last a long time. The materials and lubricant used make a huge difference to the life span of your bearings. So, when you are choosing your bearings, you are better off sticking with bearings that are made with inline skating in mind. That doesn't mean though, that you shouldn't go and pick up some dirt cheap ABEC 3s. If the bearing turns then you can skate on it.

Ceramic Bearings

A fully ceramic bearing means that there is no steel. The balls and both the inner and outer races are made of a ceramic material. This can make the bearings up to 40% lighter and deal with frictional heat better. For a skater, this is mostly unimportant. The important factors are that there is no metal to rust and cause ceasing up after a rainy skate, but also that due to being made of a more brittle material the chances of a ceramic bearing breaking on impact are higher.

Not all ceramic bearings are fully ceramic. If a bearing is referred to as 'ceramic' it may also mean that only the balls are ceramic and the race is still made of steel. For many industrial purposes this is useful as their lightness enables them to spin faster without causing problems. For skaters it means that the bearings will last longer due to the balls being harder and smoother than the metal ones since it is usually the balls which become damaged by dirt in the bearings, which then pass on the damage to the inner and outer races. The metal races will still be subject to rust, so will need the same care as a normal bearing.

Cleaning your bearings

Whether or not you choose to prolong the life of your bearings by regular cleaning is a choice that you are likely to make approximately half way through your first bearing cleaning session! Occasionally you'll meet someone that claims to have made it into a quick and effective task, but usually you'll find that you have just misunderstood what they said, and that they were actually saying how much they *wished* it was a quick and effective task.

If you decide to give it a go, you can find plenty of instructions and advice on the internet. Here is the general gist to give you an idea:

1. Lay out a large mat, put some music on, buy some drinks and snacks and invite your friends and their bearings around to your place. This is the most important part of the process.
2. Remove any bearing shells.
3. Remove the lubricant and dirt. This usually involves a solvent and lots of shaking and/or brushing with an old toothbrush.
4. Leave the bearings to dry.
5. Re-lubricate the bearings with a few drops of oil and pop the shells back on.

The solvent and lubricants that you use are not all that important. Get some white spirit and some general purpose lubricating oil from your local hardware store and you're all set. There are some odd pieces of advice that you'll come across along the way, but you should take them all with a pinch of salt and experiment with them if you wish. For example, I like to skate in the rain so I also like to inject grease between each ball bearing using a dental syringe before adding a couple of drops of oil because I think it stops them rusting as easily. Someone else I did a bearing cleaning session with once liked to melt petroleum jelly into the bearings.

All in all, cleaning your bearings is a great money saver and everyone should try it at least once, but you may decide to ride increasingly degrading bearings if you feel that it's not worth the hassle of doing again.

Common Misconceptions

Let's get some of these flushed out of the way:
- **Your bearings have come to the end of their life.** Noisy or seized bearings are not necessarily dead. If your wheels have stopped turning because you skated in the rain and left them overnight, then just go right ahead and put

them on and try to force them to skate for you. You'll be amazed at how they will eventually move for you and how fine they feel after a few miles.
- **A bearing that spins well is a good and healthy bearing.** No. Bearings that spin well without the weight of a person on them are bearings that spin well without the weight of a person on them and probably also have a very thin lubricant in them. When your body weight is being put through the bearing, particularly when it is all your body weight through just one wheel, it is a totally different story.

So, now that you've read about bearings, there is no need to talk about them ever again!

Heel Brakes

Whatever your level, it is preferable to not wear a heel brake for slalom. It gets in the way and is more likely to knock over cones or trip you up than it is to ever be useful in stopping. Slalom is rarely done on a slope, and you never need to stop during slalom. Slalom is a useful tool for learning how to change direction, and changing direction is usually a far better solution than actually stopping when trying to avoid a nasty collision.

However, many people are not psychologically ready to let go of the comfort of wearing a heel brake, and many simply don't want to go through the annoyance of removing their brake for slalom, only to have to put it back on when it's time to skate home, down those steep hills filled with cars and pushchairs.

This is fine.

If you want to wear a heel brake whilst you slalom, just be aware that it might get in the way a little, but do it anyway. Ignore everyone who tells you that you 'absolutely must take it off' – as you learn your slalom tricks you will find that you automatically adjust to giving one foot a little more room, just like you adjust when performing crossovers with speed skates on without knocking your skates together.

Customisation

Over time the skates on the market have become increasingly more suitable for slalom, and now there are various styles of skates which have been made with slalom in mind, resulting in less of a need for customising your skates. However you might feel the need to make changes to your boots to make them feel more comfortable, for example, switching the liner or changing the cuff. You also might want to upgrade the frame if you've chosen a less slalom specific boot.

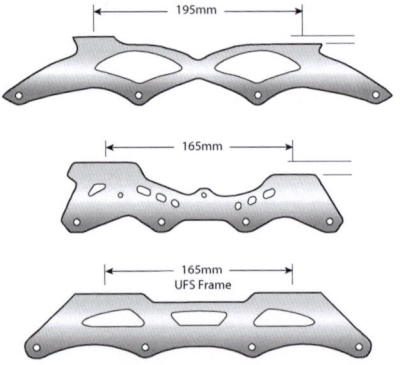

Equipment   25

When switching frames, take note of how far apart the bolts are. Most freestyle boots and frames have their bolts 165mm apart, but some speed setups are 195mm apart, so if you're looking to use any speed frames or boots, make sure they are compatible.

Most freestyle boots and frames are stepped (the heel is higher than the toe) as are speed boots and frames. This isn't the case for all skates and frames however, so don't assume before you've checked!

If you're looking to change your liner for a more comfortable one, do what you can to check the sizing. Be aware that different brands have slightly different shapes and sizes, just like buying shoes.

Protection

Level of risk

The term 'appropriate protective equipment' is usually associated with particular activities. For some activities you protect yourself, and some activities you don't. It doesn't seem to matter what risk level you're exposing yourself to within that activity, since people who have no knowledge prescribe the protection expectations of what particular risk level you personally are going to choose to do.

For example, we're all expected to wear cycle helmets, whether or not we are riding a BMX on a vert ramp, competing in an international cycle race, commuting across a congested city centre, cycling down a main road, or perhaps taking a lazy little trip through the country tracks on a short cut to the next village.

There is also little concession given for when you're not at the risk from others. My driving instructor always used to hammer in 'it's not you that's the main danger – it's the others on the road – you need to expect them to behave dangerously', and he was absolutely right. Arguably my most physically damaging skating accident was because someone who was drafting me clipped my skates. When you're taking part in an activity away from the possibility of suffering as a result of errors made by others, you're much better equipped to judge the risk of what you're doing, based on your own level.

The level of risk that you take is a product of the probability of a consequence, and the seriousness of that consequence. The consequence of a sky-dive going wrong is most probably death. The probability of that happening is absolutely tiny because of the equipment and procedures. So, I recently found myself jumping out of a plane for the first time, and no one had mentioned helmets.

In skating, when you're on inlines, diving into a ramp, you're likely to hit your head when you fall. In speed skating, if you hit your head when you fall, due to your speed, you'll probably hit it quite hard. In slalom, if you fall forward, you're massively unlikely to hit your head. If you fall backward, your hands, elbows, backside are all most likely to stop your head hitting. If your head does hit, it is unlikely to hit hard enough to cause any real damage. Bleeding? Sure. Pain? Definitely. That feeling of vulnerability and the need to cry? Almost always. But the chances of anything worse are very small indeed.

How much risk are you happy with?

Choosing the appropriate level of protection is down to balancing the level of risk of the activity against the inconvenience of protecting yourself against that risk. If we could press a button to ensure that our head would be protected in the event of a car accident, we would probably press it each time we got in a car. In a way that's what we do by having cars with airbags in them. Would we put on a helmet though? No, we probably wouldn't, because even in the pre-airbag days, we simply didn't want to. Clearly there was a risk of death from head injury, or we wouldn't have developed airbags, but not enough probability of that consequence to warrant the inconvenience and discomfort of wearing a helmet.

If you have children at home who depend on you, the consequence of your death is far greater than if you didn't, and so many people find themselves starting to wear helmets when they enter parenthood. It's all a balance. My levels of protection vary with my mood and habit, but for a general idea:

- Speed skating alone: nothing.
- Speed skating with others: helmet.
- Skating on a vert ramp: helmet and big kneepads.
- Skating on other, less fast ramps: helmet and slim kneepads, possibly with elbow and wrist pads too.
- Slalom normally: nothing
- Slalom when practising 1-wheeled tricks: hand-sliders.
- If there was anything in the world that I could wear to protect my neck against whiplash, I believe I would wear it anytime I was on a ramp, or practising 1-wheeled slalom tricks, however inconvenient and annoying it was.

Awareness of the consequences of your choices

When it all goes wrong, it can be serious. Many skaters have not quite considered the consequences of what could go wrong, and ended up with feelings of regret, and have only begun to wear appropriate protective equipment after a nasty fall. Don't let this happen to you. The most common injuries that protective gear can help prevent go something along the lines of:

- **Hitting your head** – it feels horrible and frightening, and that's when there's no real permanent damage. I've never known someone suffering permanent damage when slaloming, but since you can kill yourself by slipping on a spillage (whilst in shoes) I'm sure it must only be a matter of time.
- **Knocking your elbows** – it can permanently screw them up like mine – I have a hole in one of them that's made it impossible to lean on it for over 10 years now.
- **Knees** – I remember someone falling onto an old-style very rigid cone with sharp corner and breaking his kneecap into four pieces.
- **Wrists** – the most common injury when skating apparently – think how it would affect your work if you broke one. I think the 'heels' of my hands are permanently messed up from all the impacts.
- **Cosmetic - scars, dead teeth etc.**… I have a brilliant one just below my lower lip when my front tooth went through it during a nasty face-plant in a midi-ramp many years ago – that couldn't have been prevented using the usual protective equipment, but you need to decide if you're willing to have ugly white patches on your knees and elbows before you go out without knee and elbow pads.

So, think about how you feel about those consequences, and measure them up against how likely it is that they will happen to you. Make sure that any decision not to wear protective gear is an informed one, and won't result in you feeling like a wronged victim if probability doesn't go your way. Make sure that you know the choice you are making, and that in the event you are injured, it will have been worth feeling the wind in your hair, or being able to comfortably bend your elbows, or even just being able to answer your phone easily.

Types of protection available

The usual equipment used by skaters consists of wrist protectors, elbow pads, knee pads and helmets.

Wrist protectors – the most scuffed bit of equipment that skaters have. Freestylers will use their hands almost every time they fall. The most common ones available are wrist guards, but I recommend having a look at hand-sliders. They just provide padding and a hard plastic shell to the palm of the hand, and don't prevent the wrist joint from flexing at all. They protect the wrist not by transferring the force to the forearm, but by reducing the friction between the palm of the hand and the floor, encouraging the hand to slide on impact with the floor. This removes the jolt to the wrist.

Kneepads – highly recommended since the options available nowadays for non-annoying knee protection are much better than they used to be. I recommend a slim pad (you're not going to be taking much force, since freestyle is low speed, low height) with or without a hard shell. You might still bruise your knee, so use a larger pad if you want to feel nothing but a bruised ego when you fall. I do recommend wearing pads underneath your pants/trousers instead of over the top of them. Own one pair that you're willing to sacrifice. In slalom you're unlikely to seriously injure a pair of jeans, and it stops them from bunching up underneath your pads, either restricting your knee-bend, or giving yourself lovely knickerbockers. It also looks seriously bad. I can comfortably fit my kneepads under even my tightest jeans.

Elbow pads – same as for kneepads – though I'd recommend ones that you need to pull up over your hands, as they will be more comfortable than ones that you can just strap straight on. Again, I recommend wearing them underneath any clothing, but with elbow pads it's almost purely for cosmetic reasons, since there's little need to be using your elbows much.

Helmets – I don't want to enter the debate about the effectiveness of helmets - there's plenty of research out there supporting both sides of that debate, so I'll just feed the information about the types of helmets available. There are 3 main types:

- Cycle helmet – personally I think cycle helmets should be used for speed skating and cycling, and not for aggressive or freestyle skating. The reasons are based on the type of fall that you're likely to sustain, and the ability of each type of helmet to protect against that fall.
- Skate helmets with polystyrene inner – these are moulded polystyrene on the inside, with a thin layer of very low density foam to aid comfort. I strongly dislike these. Maybe my head is the wrong shape, but they seem to sit on top annoyingly, and bounce up and down annoyingly if the chinstrap is slightly loose, and if it's tight, then the helmet feels hard against your head. As far as I'm aware, they are the only ones available in the UK.
- Skate helmets with high density foam inner – next to the shell, they have a very high density foam layer, about 1cm thick, and then inside that, a slightly lower density foam. I love these. They fit the head snugly, and even if the strap is undone you can hang your head upside down, shaking it violently, and the helmet won't budge. A very non-annoying, comfy helmet, but unfortunately not legal to sell in the UK, so I buy mine in the USA.

GETTING READY

Choosing and Setting up your Area *31*
    Location
    Cones
    The Cone Line(s)
    Measuring Instruments

Body Conditioning *33*
    Flexibility and Stretching
    Strength and Cardiovascular Fitness

Lessons *33*
    What an instructor can give you
    Are lessons for you?
    Qualifications
    How to get the most out of instruction

Learning Tricks From Videos *37*

GETTING READY

Choosing and Setting up your Area

Location

Most people will feel strongly about skating somewhere either very private or very public. A private area is nice if you feel self-conscious, but a more public area will increase your chances of developing a local freestyle slalom scene.

Here are some considerations when choosing a location to set-up:
- Surface Texture
- Surface slope
- Surface grip in wet weather (or is it covered?)
- Likelihood of eviction
- Evening lighting?
- Safe to put your bag down?
- A cone line is about 16m long, but you don't need that much room – you can learn a lot in a garage.

If you start feeling like there is nowhere close to you that fits the bill, bear in mind that in London the skaters practise on a very rough surface that eats wheels, is on a sideways slope and has no lighting or cover. At night the skaters go to a central tourist spot with ridges between the paving slabs, and with drunks and phone users regularly kicking over their cones. In Korea the top skaters in the world often skate in Seoul's Olympic Park on small, loose tiles with ridges between them. It is very unusual to find the perfect skating spot.

Cones

Cones have come a long way since the days of international competitions featuring upturned IKEA picnic cups as the official standard! There are various types of slalom cones available to us now, with various advantages and disadvantages. Here is the lowdown on the important factors when selecting objects to set down in a neat, orderly line:

- **Resistance to wind (if skating outdoors)** – You don't want your cones flying away in the wind. Cones tend to do that. It is generally down to their weight and their shape.
- **Stackability** – closely stacking cones are much more convenient than the old picnic cup style ones that we used to use.
- **Hardness** – Too hard and horrendous pain and bruising will result from falling on them. Too soft and although they will collapse easily, leaving no bruises

on their victims, they will sometimes deform to allow the offending wheel to ride over it slightly. This results in the skate stopping dead, leading to some very nasty falls, particularly if travelling backward, or on one wheel. Harder cones will rebound away from any wheel that knocks it. The more popular cones nowadays are those which strike a happy medium between these two extremes.
- **Toughness** – Cones receive an absolute punishing. Whether it is from skaters falling on them or from the random acts of our companions in the human race, a set of 20 cones can become a set of 14 cones surprisingly quickly if they are too brittle.
- **Size** – Smaller cones are easier to use, larger ones are more difficult. I used to have a set of larger cones for practice just before competitions.

If you don't have easy access to any of the slalom cones available on the market, and upturned picnic cups fly away from you, feel free to make your own. It's unlikely that you'll come up with anything weirder than some of the solutions that have already been seen – decapitated traffic cones, used wheels, crushed (or uncrushed) drinks cans … the list goes on.

The Cone Line(s)

There are three cone spacings that we use in competition and normal skating:
- 50cm
- 80cm
- 120cm

The middle distance, 80cm spacing, is the one that is used most often and therefore almost exclusively in most freestyle slalom videos you will see.

There are usually 20 cones in a line, except for the 120cm line which has 14 cones. When laying out, try to allow enough space at either end for any run-up or run-off needed for faster tricks.

If you set up somewhere new and there are regular sized paving slabs on the floor, measure them. If they are somewhere between 75cm and 90cm, then they should be fine to use as cone spacers. It is easy to worry a little too much about cone spacing. We'll often just roll up somewhere new, set up a line by eye, and skate them until the line has got so distorted that it needs picking up and laying again from scratch.

Measuring Instruments

If you need to measure out the space of your cones every time you slalom, then you'll want a quick and easy method of doing so. There are currently two good ways of doing this:

1. Use a coloured marker pen to mark 80cm on a measuring tape. When using a 9m measuring tape for marking 80cm spots, mark 11 dots, and then pull the tape along for another 9 dots.

2. Tie knots in, or mark in another way, a piece of non-creasing string. It is very important that the material you use does not crinkle up, or you'll need people to help you hold the string straight and taut.

Body Conditioning

Flexibility and Stretching

Freestyle slalom skaters often don't stretch much, as it isn't a sport that requires flexibility outside of a few tricks such as sitting tricks and those that require your hips to be very open or closed such as Eagle and Butterfly, where the feet point outwards, and Inverted Eagle, where the feet point inwards. Other than those special cases, surprisingly little flexibility is needed. It may look like the legs bend in impossible ways, but that isn't the case at all.

To use the example of myself, I cannot do the Eagle and I can barely stand with my feet pointing in at a right angle to each other, but when I skate it looks as if my feet are achieving some extreme positions. Freestyle slalom is like sleight of hand with the feet – what you think you're seeing is not usually the reality. The reality is usually much physically easier and more accessible than you would imagine.

Strength and Cardiovascular Fitness

No initial cardiovascular fitness is needed beyond what you need in order to skate slowly in a straight line. For competitions you do need a certain amount of cardiovascular fitness but it is a specific fitness that you will get from doing it. There is more information on this in the Preparing for Competitions chapter (p 121).

The relevant muscles usually develop from practising skills and tricks anyway, so there is no need for additional strength training. Developing core strength is always a winner though, and it is always a good idea to supplement your freestyle skating with some yoga or Pilates – they stretch pretty much every muscle in the body and keep you flexible as well as developing core strength.

Lessons

A popular opinion among freestyle slalom skaters who have never taken a lesson is that there is not usually a need for an instructor or coach when you can learn from fellow skaters. This is only true if your instructor has no specific training in the teaching and coaching of freestyle slalom. There is a lot more to creating great slalomers than imparting tricks. For the simplicity of using just one word, the term 'instructor' is used here to also cover coaching roles such as guiding and shaping a top competitor to excellence.

What an instructor can give you

A qualified slalom instructor can give you so much more than you would initially expect, and I have always enjoyed the amazement of new students that initially came to a class to 'learn a new trick' or 'learn with others' when they see how much more they are gaining.

There is considerably more to teaching slalom than communicating where the feet go during specific tricks. A qualified instructor should be able to treat your entire body as one mechanism, improving flow, speed, power and any other quality you want to change. They can help you work out a path to being able to do the tricks that you're aiming for. Rarely will they need to tell you to 'just practise it until it comes' because there are usually skill-based exercises which can help you accelerate towards your goal with less head-against-a-brick-wall style practice.

An instructor will also be able to take a look at your skating or your tricks and be able to solve the problems you are having with tricks that you're learning. I've always wanted a coach, and now I never miss an opportunity to attend workshops run by my students that I've since certified as slalom instructors – I love the indulgence of having someone else looking at my tricks from the outside and being able to tell me what is happening each time I fall out of a trick.

Are lessons for you?

Despite the definite and significant advantages to taking lessons, they might not be for you. Some people just want to be left alone to learn in their own way, at their own pace. Freestyle slalom skating may be a 'sport', but to most of us it is a hobby, a pastime, an outlet for self-expression, and although a greater skill level will increase your ability to express yourself as you wish, the enjoyment is in the journey, in the practice, in the meditation of endless repetitions and in the joy of tiny achievements along the path of learning.

Sometimes I don't even want to accept tips from anyone when learning something new, and I want to just be able to ask questions when I want. In recent years I would often get lesson-hating self-teachers to my workshops – they come along and just want to be able to ask questions, and use me as a resource to help them solve their own problems. Everyone learns and enjoys in different ways, so just go with what works best for you.

Qualifications

There are many skating instructor qualifications in existence in the world. The principle two types are national and international.

Many countries have their own 'national' general skating qualifications, and these are usually designed for instructors that will work in schools or with large groups of children, bringing them into the sport. They are usually not very good for the actual teaching of skating, and certainly not what you are after if you have bought this book.

There are two actual skating instructor certifications in the world which, at the time of print, still operate independently of national federations. These are the ICP (Inline Certification Program) and SkateIA (Skate Instructor Association). They used to both be ICP and operate under the IISA (International Inline Skating Association) until the IISA disbanded in 2004 at which point the ICP split into 'USA' and 'Non-USA', with SkateIA being the USA program.

At the time of print, the only specifically slalom instructor training and certification programmes are with the ICP – the ICP Slalom Instructor Program, and with Skate IA. Whatever your level, taking slalom classes from an instructor who is not specifically trained to teach slalom will be a completely different experience to taking classes from an instructor who has received training in teaching slalom.

How to get the most out of instruction

Your instructor will not expect you have done any preparation before showing up to a lesson.

However if you want the time to be as tailored to your specific needs as possible, try to give some thought to:
- what your aims are;
- what you enjoy about slalom;
- your reason for taking a lesson;
- what well known skater(s) you would like to skate like; and
- any specific tricks or type of tricks that you would love to learn – however ambitious.

Then spill all of this out to your instructor. If it is a group class, try to do this before the start of the lesson.

You are paying your instructor, and they are providing a service to you – they are working for you and they want you to get what you want and need out of the lesson. Always remember this. The instructor's job is to help you reach your goals by guiding you through what you need to do. Teaching slalom is not the industry to be in if you're after the big bucks, so every instructor that is offering specifically slalom instruction is no doubt doing it out of a love for the sport and will enjoy catering to your specific needs.

Sometimes they might totally overrule what you think you want, and give you instead something you never realised you wanted – they might say 'no' to the tricks you want, and instead make you do something which feels completely below your level, and only at the end of the session will you realise the significant effect that it has had on the flow of your slalom – which you asked them at the start to help you improve.

The instructor can only do so much however, and it is up to you to put their coaching to work. They cannot give you skills – they can only guide you through the process of what you need to do to gain them for yourself. You must back up lessons with plenty of practice. If you are taking regular lessons then make sure you do at least one hour's practice for every hour of instruction. If you are just taking a one-off lesson make sure your instructor knows that, and they will give you a long list of homework to keep you going for a good long time.

Learning Tricks From Videos

When learning new tricks, getting the feet to roll in the correct pattern on the ground can seem like the only important thing. If only life were that simple. Learning the correct path of the skates is only the beginning. There are many other things that you will need to watch out for in order to execute the trick successfully.

Make sure you also know which edges your wheels need to be on, which foot your weight should be on, whether your weight should be at the front, middle or back of each skate. Take a look at the positions of the hips, the shoulders, the head. Do the arms need to be used in order to make the trick work? Are either of the feet used as air-borne counterbalances?

Your body is a simple mechanism which relies on all of these being correct in order to operate the same as the person on the screen. Here is a checklist of things to watch:

Checklist of Things to Watch

Head	❑ Which way is it facing? ❑ Where is the skater looking?
Arms	❑ Are they being used for the trick to work?
Shoulders	❑ Which direction are they facing? ❑ Rounded or back?
Hips	❑ Which direction is the pelvis facing? ❑ Angled up or down?
Knees	❑ Are they bent enough? ❑ Are they falling in towards each other?
Torso	❑ What angle is the spine at?
Edges	❑ Are the wheels on the correct edge? ❑ Are they natural edges or rolled edges?
Weight	❑ Which foot? ❑ Where in foot?
Centre of Gravity	❑ What is its path? ❑ How high is it?
Power	❑ Where is it coming from?
Amplitude and Shape	❑ Pay attention to the amplitude and shape of the skate's path.

When watching the video, don't try to get the entire trick at once. Take just one cone or weight transition at a time and get that correct before moving onto the next one. It is a slow way of doing it but it will reduce mistakes and improve the quality of your finished trick or combo. You should put yourself in the position of the skater and imagine that you are seeing everything from their point of view. Feel what they feel, even in the strain of their muscles, as they complete each manoeuvre – this visualisation will start your muscle memory developing even before you have set foot near a cone. Once you have visualised for a cone, go and try that out on a cone set up near to your video player, even if it is just three cones set up on the carpet in your front room.

Even if you do not have a method of playing video in slow motion, you can repeatedly play the same moment again and again in quick succession at normal speed. I didn't always have a method of playing in slow motion, so I learned the tricks and style of a skater by repeatedly pausing and putting my body into the exact position I saw on the video.

FOUNDATION TRICKS

Foundation Tricks *41*

Crisscross *44*

Snake *46*

Basketweave *48*

1-Foot *50*

Nelson *52*

Back Cross *54*

Backward Snake *56*

Back 1-Foot *58*

Back Nelson *60*

Mega *62*

Sun *64*

FOUNDATION TRICKS

A book is not really the place to learn new tricks. Having said that, this chapter introduces the tricks which form the foundations of good quality slalom and a rapid learning curve. As you work through each trick in this chapter, you will be given a step-by-step approach to learning the trick, as well as advice on avoiding common problems and improving quality. There will also be tips on which tricks you should have learned before giving each trick a go, along with suggestions as to which tricks you can mix with and go onto next.

Foundation Tricks

If you are just getting started in slalom, these are the tricks that you will be using. Foundation tricks are the ones that if you practise until you have them to a really good quality, including switching between them and doing them both sides, you will be giving yourself a strong head start for learning the rest of the freestyle tricks. If you get your posture, weight transfers, smoothness and power in good shape for these tricks then those sought after qualities will automatically follow you up the scale to the more difficult tricks.

If any of your foundation tricks are weak, even on your less comfortable side, then they will be limiting the overall level and quality of your slalom. If you find any one of them to be weak, you absolutely must work on it until it is more comfortable. When you start performing difficult tricks which use only two wheels, such as the Screw, then you must re-learn all of these foundations using only those two wheels – after all you cannot possibly expect to be able to control yourself well on two wheels with your legs crossed and rotating if you cannot even control yourself on those two wheels when your legs are not crossed and not rotating.

Here are the foundation tricks which you should learn on both sides:
- **Crisscross** (Forward and Backward)
- **Snake** (Forward and Backward)
- **1-Foot** (Forward and Backward)
- **Nelson** (Forward and Backward)
- **Mega**
- **Sun**

The appearance in this list of 'Mega' and 'Sun' might surprise, however they are important for covering all of the basic transitions between forward and backward in each direction. Once all of these tricks are mastered a slalomer can survive most trips and problems while maintaining style and flow.

When you're having a go at them, ask yourself the following questions for each one:
- **Form:** Is my upper body in a good posture? (see notes for each trick)
- **Fluidity**: Is it free flowing? Or does it feel hesitant and slow?

- **Smoothness:** Does my centre of gravity travel along at a constant velocity?
- **Power:** Are my leg muscles really working? How wide is the path made by my skates? Are my arms and upper body working together with my legs as one body?
- Can I do it both sides?
- Can I easily switch between this trick and the other foundation tricks?

If the answer to any of the above questions is 'no', I strongly suggest spending time solidifying these foundations as you will be rewarded with a faster learning curve later on. If you are already a very advanced slalomer then revisiting these foundations and working on any problems that you find will help you with the more advanced tricks that you might be struggling with.

It is always advisable to learn all tricks on both sides. However it is not usually detrimental to the level of your slalom if you don't do this with the more advanced tricks. With these foundation tricks, however, it is.

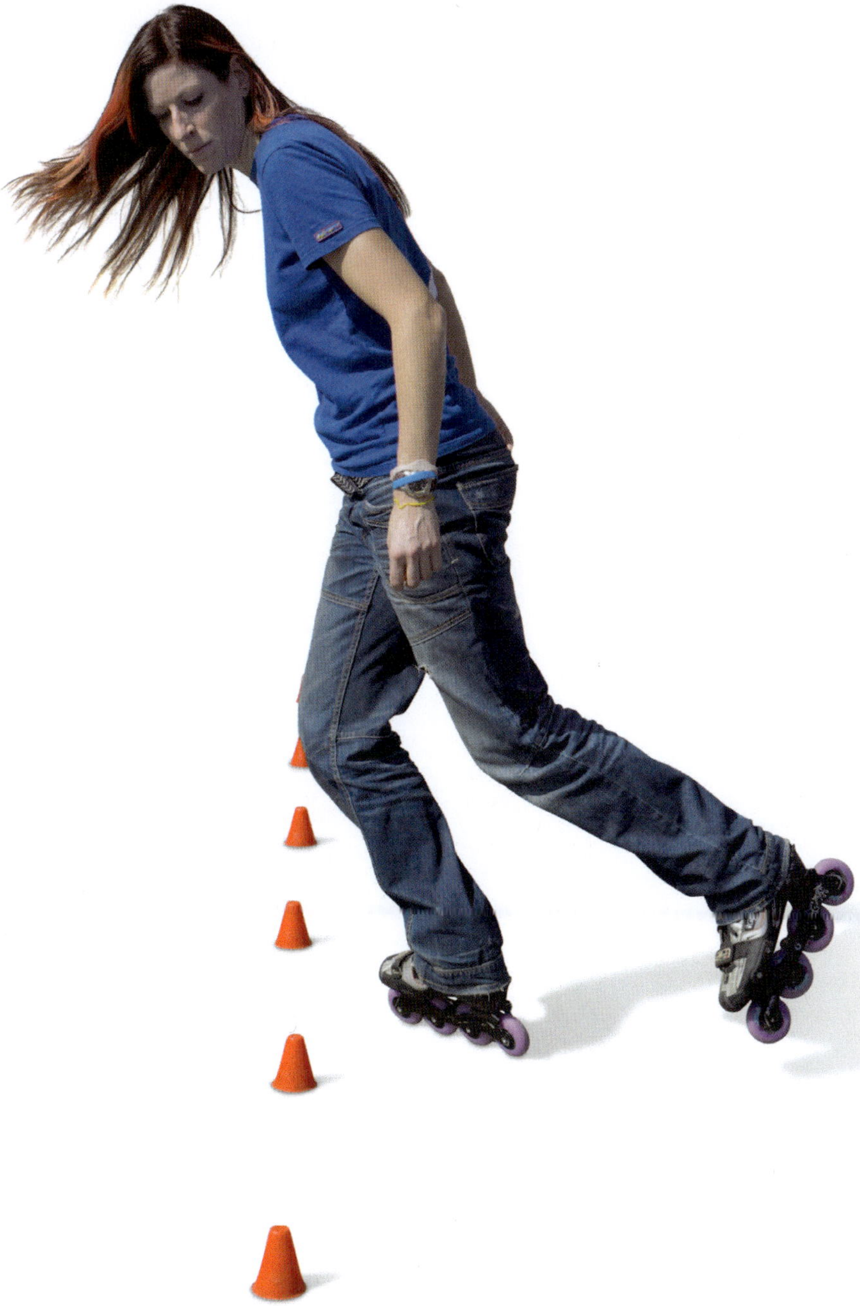

CRISSCROSS

Crisscross is the first classic freestyle slalom trick. Also it is probably the most rewarding trick to learn for the feel good factor, as you do things that previously may have seemed impossible, and you will also find that flexibility is not important! Crisscross has a 2 cone cycle.

Step by Step Approach to Learning It

- You will only be crossing every other cone, so do a lemon/swizzle over the first cone.
- Once you have passed the 1st cone, get your skates onto their outside edges if they are not already on them.
- To cross the 2nd cone, transfer more weight onto the foot that you would like to lead. This should cause your feet to cross.
- Once past the cone, transfer weight back onto the trailing foot, allowing the lead foot to uncross.
- Lemon/swizzle the 3rd cone to start the cycle again.

Complementary Tricks

Previous tricks to have learned:
- Snake (or none)

Tricks you should consider next:
- Basketweave
- Backward Crisscross
- 1-Foot

Tricks it mixes well with:
- Snake
- Backward Crisscross

CRISSCROSS

Tips on Style and Flow

Notes on correct posture
Forward crisscross is one of the most awkward tricks to do, and it can show unless effort is made to relax the arms, keep the hips low and tucked under and keep the torso upright.

Where weight should be
Your weight should be towards the backs of the skates, allowing maximum manoeuvrability. Weight can either switch back and forth between the two feet (lead foot when crossing, trailing foot when uncrossing) or remain equal on each foot.

What the centre of mass should be doing
The centre of mass should be travelling along above the line of cones, at a constant speed, direction and height.

How to create power and energy
The feet should make as wide a path as possible. Also change the direction of the feet as quickly and aggressively as possible - pull the feet apart when uncrossing, and thrust them across each other when crossing.

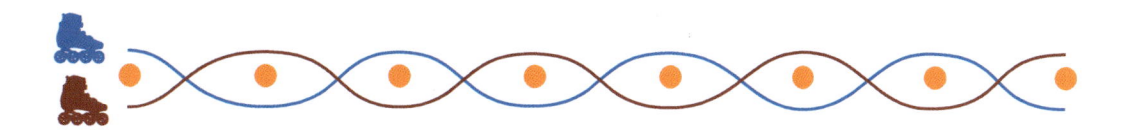

Troubleshooting of Common Problems

Not having enough space to cross and uncross (the cones feel too close together).
Cross and uncross immediately after each cone, and make sure that your weight is towards the heels of the feet. This will be easier if your posture is good, with hips forward and torso upright.

Feet collide instead of crossing.
Keep hips low, feet on outside edges, and weight on the leading foot whilst crossing.

Feet don't want to uncross.
Make sure that the skates are on their outside edges and the weight has transferred onto the trailing foot. Also make sure the hips are forward and the torso is upright. You can also try lifting the toe of the lead foot to aid uncrossing in the short term, or drag your lead skate across the floor instead of rolling it – this will eventually evolve into a rolling uncross. DO NOT pick up any foot to aid uncrossing, since this will not evolve into a rolling uncross.

SNAKE

Snake is a difficult trick for new slalomers to get right and it gets a lot easier after learning Crisscross. Make it big!

Step by Step Approach to Learning It

- Give yourself enough runup so that your feet are completely in line (not scissoring).
- Skates slightly on the outside edges.
- Slalom between the cones, keeping the skates tracing the same wide, monoline path as each other for the entire line.
- The trailing foot can take more weight than the leading foot, allowing the leading foot to do most of the work.
- The feet, particularly the front foot, must push not only on the inside edge turn, but also the outside edge turn.

Complementary Tricks

Previous tricks to have learned:
- Crisscross (or none)

Tricks you should consider next:
- CrissCross
- Back Snake
- 1-Foot

Tricks it mixes well with:
- Crisscross
- Back Snake
- Push

SNAKE

Tips on Style and Flow

Notes on correct posture
Forward slalom tricks can be quite awkward for the legs and hips – our body accommodates the backward ones more naturally, since our ankles are at the backs of the feet, and our knees point forward. As a result, extra care needs to be taken to ensure that the hips are kept low and tucked under and that the torso is upright. Also be aware of what your arms are doing – focus on relaxing them.

Where weight should be
Your weight should be towards the backs of the skates, and mostly on the trailing foot, to allow the leading foot to explore a more side-to-side, exaggerated path.

What the centre of mass should be doing
The centre of mass should be travelling along above the line of cones, at a constant speed, direction and height.

How to create power and energy
The feet should make as wide a path as possible whilst still travelling along the same monoline – it will often feel as if you are doing Crisscross without crossing any cones. If your centre of mass deviates from side to side slightly in the name of power, then that's fine. Also, try thrusting the front foot forward and across when it crosses over to the opposite side of the cones, and pulling it hard when it returns to its own side.

Troubleshooting of Common Problems

Feet pushing only on their inside edges.
The feet should always push just as hard on their outside edge turn as their inside edge turn. It will also be the front foot that does most of these pushes.

Feet travelling along two separate parallel lines.
This is not 'Fish with One Foot Sightly in Front', nor is this 'Scissor'. This is 'Snake' – make sure that your feet roll along the same line as each other.

Feet too connected to each other.
This looks stiff and awkward – sit down a little lower to give the feet more scope, and separate them a little more along the snaking path so they are at least one skate-length apart and clearly moving at different phases of the cycle.

The Art of Falling: Freestyle Slalom Skating

BASKETWEAVE

Basketweave is just Crisscross but with the lead foot alternating each cycle - each time the feet cross a cone, it is with a different foot. Many people find it easier than doing Crisscross on their more difficult side. Basketweave has a 4-cone cycle.

Step by Step Approach to Learning It

- The 1st and 2nd cones as per Crisscross.
- When lemoning/swizzling over the 3rd cone, keep the weight on the foot which was the trailing foot causing it to take over as the lead foot when you come out of the lemon and cross your feet for the 4th cone.
- Uncross your feet after the 4th cone and lemon/swizzle the 5th to start the cycle again.

Complementary Tricks

Previous tricks to have learned:
- Crisscross
- Crisscross switch (on your less natural side)

Tricks you should consider next:
- Backward Crisscross

Tricks it mixes well with:
- Swinging Basketweave
- Forward-Backward Transitions

BASKETWEAVE

Tips on Style and Flow

Notes on correct posture
As with Crisscross, relax the arms, keep the hips low and tucked under and keep the torso upright. You might want to swing the arms a little, but it is hard to make it natural – arm swing is best left for 'Swinging Basketweave' where there is more side-to-side movement.

Where weight should be
Your weight should be towards the backs of the skates, allowing maximum manoeuvrability. Weight can either switch back and forth between the two feet (lead foot when crossing, trailing foot when uncrossing), or remain equal on each foot. If switching then there is no weight transfer between the cones (like in Crisscross) there is only a weight transfer when crossing over the cones.

What the centre of mass should be doing
The centre of mass should be travelling along above the line of cones, at a constant speed, direction and height.

How to create power and energy
The feet should make as wide a path as possible. Also change the direction of the feet as quickly and aggressively as possible - pull the feet apart when uncrossing, and thrust them across each other when crossing.

Troubleshooting of Common Problems

Problems crossing or uncrossing, or not having enough space.
See the troubleshooting section for Crisscross.

Not knowing where to switch the lead foot.
The lead foot should change when the feet are lemoning/swizzling a cone.

1-FOOT

1-Foot slalom is not just a speed slalom trick. Whether or not you think it has a place in freestyle slalom combos that you want to be able to do, you must learn this trick. It is working on your skills of being able to balance and gain control on one skate. This will greatly improve your ease of movement and speed through the cones.

Step by Step Approach to Learning It

- Skate along, lift up one foot.
- Transfer weight towards the back of the foot.
- Use any combination of arm/leg swinging and edge switching to move the skate from side to side, slaloming the cones.
- There is no strict method for 1-Foot – see what feels right for you.

Complementary Tricks

Previous tricks to have learned:
- Snake or Crisscross

Tricks you should consider next:
- 1-Foot Backward
- Nelson

Tricks it mixes well with:
- Basketweave
- 1-Foot switch (on your less natural side)

1-FOOT

Tips on Style and Flow

Notes on correct posture
Keep as much of your body mass centred around the central line of your body as possible, so no leaning over. This can be a tough balance trick whilst learning it, so the arms must be watched! Do not let them fly around, try to keep them relaxed and swinging.

Where weight should be
The weight should be towards the back of the foot.

What the centre of mass should be doing
The centre of mass should be travelling along above the line of cones, at a constant speed, direction and height.

How to create power and energy
Try increasing your speed during the line of cones by pumping each turn, getting a real push out of it. You can bend your knee whilst going into each turn, and then straighten it as you turn.

Troubleshooting of Common Problems

Running out of speed.
Check that your weight is not too far forward. Also check that your skate is very close to being on its centre edge – too much edge will create friction with the ground.

Can only turn the foot one way.
Usually people have no problem turning their foot towards the centre of their body. Turning the foot away from the centre of the body is much harder, since if we overbalance there is no other foot easily at hand to land on. You must therefore consciously encourage your skate to lean onto the outside edge, and your centre of mass to lean slightly to the outside of the foot, to encourage the foot to roll over to the other side and save you from falling.

NELSON

The skills and movements developed in Nelson are key parts of almost all other slalom tricks. It can feel like an unnatural contortion at the start, but that is just a sign that the body/feet interaction and coordination that it grows have not yet been developed.

Step by Step Approach to Learning It

For moving toward your left ('Regular' direction for snowboarders and skateboarders):

- Draw a sideways facing V between cones 1 and 2, between 3 and 4 and so on. i.e. in every other space.
- Start in a sideways facing V shape, between cones 1 and 2. You will have the cone line extending toward your left, and your heels will be together, toes apart.

Step 1: Pick up right foot and step behind left foot, with cone between the feet. Both feet now pointing same direction.

Step 2: Roll left foot around the cone as your body rotates anti clockwise. Feet end up in a V facing the direction of the cone line.

Step 3: Clockwise forward uncrossed heel pivot using right heel, but the heel comes off of the ground instead of pivoting.

Complementary Tricks

Previous tricks to have learned:
- Crisscross

Tricks you should consider next:
- Backward Nelson
- Backward Crisscross
- Sun

Tricks it mixes well with:
- Sun
- Mega
- Crisscross

NELSON

Tips on Style and Flow

Notes on correct posture
The ability of your feet to do this move well depends upon the behaviour of your upper body. Shoulders will face the direction of travel, while the hips rotate about 90 degrees each cone. They will vary between facing the direction of travel, and facing the side, perpendicular to the direction of travel. To help:
- Work on your arm swing as it will greatly help or hinder this. Check out videos to help.
- Keep your torso upright in order to enable that hip rotation.

Where weight should be
Your weight is on the foot that never leaves the ground. However you will apply a fair amount of pressure to the swinging foot in order to generate the forward motion, as it pushes sideways from the line while being at an angle, almost like a fish's tail generating motion through water.

What the centre of mass should be doing
The centre of mass will experience a very slight rhythmic up/down motion and constant speed in the forward direction.

How to create power and energy
- increase the armswing
- Increase the amplitude of the snaking foot. This will force more significant hip rotation and make every movement stronger and more powerful
- Increase length that the swinging foot spends in contact with the ground.

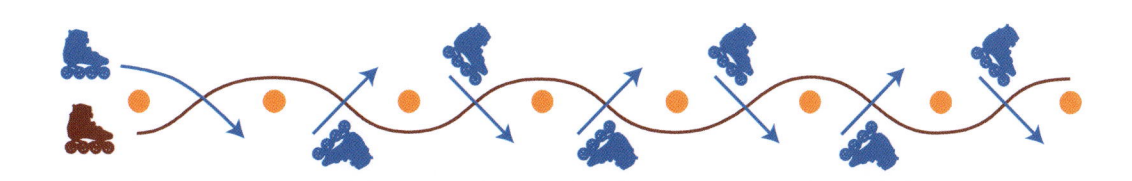

Troubleshooting of Common Problems

Snake Nelson
Do both of your skates pass the same side of each cone as each other? Yes? You're doing the Snake Nelson, which is not rich in the skills that you're trying to develop. Ensure right from the start that your feet are always on opposite sides of each cone.

Swinging foot always pointing forward and never back
Follow posture tips above to help you to rotate your hips more to the side. Foot motion is full of effort and driven by wiggling the hips.

Lack of forward energy
The swinging foot is probably almost always perpendicular to the cone line. The foot needs to be at an angle in order for its contact with the ground to generate any forward movement. The closer the angle to the cone line, the more difficult the stroke will be but the more forward movement will be generated, just like gears on a bike.

BACK CROSS

Back Cross can be attempted even if you are not happy with your backward skating. It can really work to improve, instead of use, your backward skills. It is easier than forward Crisscross because our body mechanics are more appropriate for it, though the aim is a lot harder because you are twisting your body to look behind you.

Step by Step Approach to Learning It

- You will only be crossing every other cone, so do a backward lemon/swizzle over the first cone.
- Once you have passed the 1st cone, get your skates onto their outside edges if they are not already on them.
- To cross the 2nd cone, transfer more weight onto the foot that you would like to lead. This should cause your feet to cross.
- Once past the cone, transfer weight back onto the trailing foot, allowing the lead foot to uncross.
- Lemon/swizzle the 3rd cone to start the cycle again.

Complementary Tricks

Previous tricks to have learned:
- Crisscross
- Backward Lemons (without cones)

Tricks you should consider next:
- Backward Nelson
- Forward-Backward Transitions
- 1-Foot

Tricks it mixes well with:
- Backward Nelson
- Crisscross
- Backward Snake

BACK CROSS

Tips on Style and Flow

Notes on correct posture
Check that your hips are pushed forward, that you are not leaning forward, and that you are looking behind you to see the cones that you are weaving between. You absolutely must be looking over the shoulder of the leading foot – do not twist your body to look over the other shoulder. Watch out for your forearms echoing the movements of your feet!

Where weight should be
Your weight should be towards the front of the skates, allowing maximum manoeuvrability. Weight can either switch back and forth between the two feet (lead foot when crossing, trailing foot when uncrossing), or remain equal on each foot.

What the centre of mass should be doing
The centre of mass should be travelling along above the line of cones, at a constant speed, direction and height.

How to create power and energy
The feet should make as wide a path as possible. Also change the direction of the feet as quickly and aggressively as possible – pull the feet apart when uncrossing, and thrust them across each other when crossing.

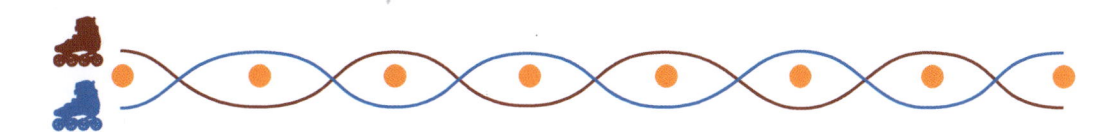

Troubleshooting of Common Problems

Not having enough space to cross and uncross (the cones feel too close together).
This is less of a problem when travelling backward, but can still happen. Cross and uncross immediately after each cone, and make sure that your weight is towards the toes of the feet. This will be easier if your posture is good, with hips forward and torso upright.

Feet collide instead of crossing.
Keep hips low, feet on outside edges, and weight on the leading foot whilst crossing.

Feet don't want to uncross.
Make sure that the skates are on their outside edges and the weight has transferred onto the trailing foot. Also make sure the hips are forward and the torso is upright. You can also try lifting the heel of the lead foot to aid uncrossing in the short term, or drag your lead skate across the floor instead of rolling it – this will eventually evolve into a rolling uncross. DO NOT pick up any foot to aid uncrossing, since this will not evolve into a rolling uncross.

Can't aim properly.
Very common – you need to recalibrate because you are twisting your body to look behind you. If you are going off to the left hand side, imagine that the cones go off to the right, and aim for them instead – then you will go straight. Soon enough your system will recalibrate and it won't be a problem anymore.

BACKWARD SNAKE

Although this seems like the most basic backward trick, it can be more challenging than Backward Crisscross, so feel free to approach these in reverse order. Backward Snake can be a very strong, flowing trick if done well and with feeling, but very limp and awkward if just 'executed' through the cones, so don't neglect this potentially beautiful trick.

Step by Step Approach to Learning It

- Turn to backward, and get a steady backward motion before entering the cones. Some people find it easier to start from standing by the cones.
- Get your skates completely in line (not scissoring).
- Skates slightly on the outside edges.
- Slalom between the cones, keeping the skates tracing the same wide, monoline path as each other for the entire line.
- The trailing foot can take more weight than the leading foot, allowing the leading foot to do most of the work.
- The feet, particularly the lead foot, must push not only on the inside edge turn, but also the outside edge turn.

Complementary Tricks

Previous tricks to have learned:
- Snake
- Backward Skating (off cones)

Tricks you should consider next:
- Backward Crisscross
- Backward 1-Foot
- Alternating Backward Snake

Tricks it mixes well with:
- Backward Snake switch (less natural side)
- Backward Crisscross
- Backward 1-Foot

BACKWARD SNAKE

Tips on Style and Flow

Notes on correct posture
Posture whilst travelling backward can be very difficult for beginner slalomers, and is absolutely vital to executing the trick successfully. Check that your hips are pushed forward, that you are not leaning forward, and that you are looking behind you to see the cones that you are weaving between. You absolutely must be looking over the shoulder of the leading foot – do not twist your body to look over the other shoulder.

Where weight should be
Weight can either be mostly on the trailing foot, allowing the lead foot to move more side to side, or alternating between the two feet every cone so that the weight is on the foot as it travels back towards the body.

What the centre of mass should be doing
The centre of mass should be travelling along above the line of cones, at a constant speed, direction and height.

How to create power and energy
- The feet should make as wide a path as possible whilst still travelling along the same monoline – it will often feel as if you are doing backward Crisscross but without crossing any cones.
- If your centre of mass deviates from side to side slightly in the name of power, then that's fine. Also, try thrusting the leading foot when it comes back underneath your body, and pulling it hard away from you when it returns to its own side.

Troubleshooting of Common Problems

Feet pushing only on their inside edges.
The feet should always push just as hard on their outside edge turn as their inside edge turn. It will also be the leading foot that does most of these pushes.

Feet travelling along two separate parallel lines.
This is not 'Backward Fish with One Foot Slightly in Front', nor is this 'Backward Scissor'. This is 'Backward Snake' – make sure that your feet roll along the same line as each other

Feet too connected to each other.
This looks stiff and awkward – sit down a little lower to give the feet more scope, and separate them a little more along the snaking path so they are at least a skate's length apart and clearly moving at different phases of the cycle.

BACK 1-FOOT

As with Forward 1-Foot, Back 1-Foot is a very important trick to learn early on in order to improve your ease of movement during more complex tricks. It works on your balance and gives you greater control of where your weight is, helping you to pick up new tricks more quickly.

Step by Step Approach to Learning It

- Skate along backward, lift up the foot on the side that you are looking over.
- Transfer weight towards the front of the skate.
- Swing the arms and 'air leg' to help move the skate from side to side, slaloming the cones.

Complementary Tricks

Previous tricks to have learned:
- Forward 1-Foot
- Backward Crisscross, Snake or Nelson

Tricks you should consider next:
- Any 1-foot transition tricks
- Backward Nelson

Tricks it mixes well with:
- Forward 1-Foot
- Backward Nelson
- Backward Snake

BACK 1-FOOT

Tips on Style and Flow

Notes on correct posture
- Keep as much of your body mass centred around the central line of your body as possible, so no leaning over. This can be a tough balance trick whilst learning it, so the arms must be watched! Don't let them fly around, try to keep them relaxed and swinging.
- Bend your 'air leg' knee and keep the 'air foot' close to the rest of you. This will help you to keep a more upright posture, and thus greater control.
- Get your 'air foot' pointing out at about 90 degrees to the line of cones.
- You MUST look over the shoulder of the 'air leg'.

Where weight should be
The weight should be towards the front of the foot.

What the centre of mass should be doing
The centre of mass should be travelling along above the line of cones, at a constant speed, direction and height.

How to create power and energy
- Try increasing your speed during the line of cones by pumping each turn, getting a real push out of it. You can bend your knee whilst going into each turn, and then straighten it as you turn.
- Use your other leg and foot as a counterbalance and swing them as you slalom the cones on the other foot. Also get your arms swinging too. To get the other limbs working, try going into this trick from Backward Nelson.

Troubleshooting of Common Problems

Running out of speed.
Check that your weight is not too far towards the heel. Also check that your skate is very close to being on its centre edge – too much edge will create friction with the ground. Leaning over can also lead to the running out of energy, because it causes a lack of control over where the weight is within the skate – pumping can't take place. Try going back to another backward trick and going into the Back 1-Foot from that.

Can only turn the foot one way.
Usually people have no problem turning their foot towards the centre of their body. Turning the foot away from the centre of the body is much harder, since if we overbalance there is no other foot easily at hand to land on. You must therefore consciously encourage your skate to lean onto the outside edge, and your centre of mass to lean slightly to the outside of the foot, to encourage the foot to roll over to the other side and save you from falling.

Foot motion is full of effort and driven by wiggling the hips.
Swing both your air leg and your arms so that the side-to-side motion of the skate is more free and natural, instead of being wiggled along, driven by twisting your torso and hips. Have a go at Backward Nelson to remind yourself of the feel and motion of the other foot.

60 **The Art of Falling:** Freestyle Slalom Skating

BACK NELSON

Backward Nelson is usually physically easier than the forward Nelson and just as drenched with key skills for other slalom tricks. It is also great for developing backward to forward transitions both in and out of cones.

Step by Step Approach to Learning It

For moving toward your left ('Regular' direction for snowboarders and skateboarders):

- Draw a sideways facing V between cones 1 and 2, between 3 and 4 and so on. i.e. in every other space.
- Start in a sideways facing V shape, between cones 1 and 2. You will have the cone line extending toward your left, and your heels will be together, toes apart.

Step 1: Clockwise backward uncrossed heel pivot using left heel, but the heel comes off the ground instead of pivoting.

Step 2: Back cross with left foot leading. Do not uncross.

Step 3: Pick up left foot and place so that your feet are in the V position, as marked.

Complementary Tricks

Previous tricks to have learned:
- Backward Crisscross

Tricks you should consider next:
- Mega
- Sun
- Backward 1-Foot

Tricks it mixes well with:
- All backward foundation tricks
- Sun
- Mega

Foundation Tricks 61

BACK NELSON

Tips on Style and Flow

Notes on correct posture
The ability of your feet to do this move well depends upon the behaviour of your upper body. Shoulders will face the side (perpendicular to the direction of travel), while the hips rotate about 90 degrees each cone. They will vary between facing away from the direction of travel, and facing the side, perpendicular to the direction of travel. To help:

- Work on your arm swing as it will greatly help or hinder this. Check out videos to help.
- Keep your torso upright in order to enable that hip rotation and allow good balance and control of the move on your skates.

Where weight should be
Your weight is on the foot that never leaves the ground. However you will apply a fair amount of pressure to the swinging foot in order to generate the forward motion, as it pushes sideways from the line while being at an angle, almost like a fish's tail generating motion through water.

What the centre of mass should be doing
The centre of mass will experience a very slight rhythmic up/down motion and constant speed in the backward direction.

How to create power and energy
- Increase the armswing
- Increase the amplitude of the snaking foot. This will force more significant hip rotation and make every movement stronger and more powerful.

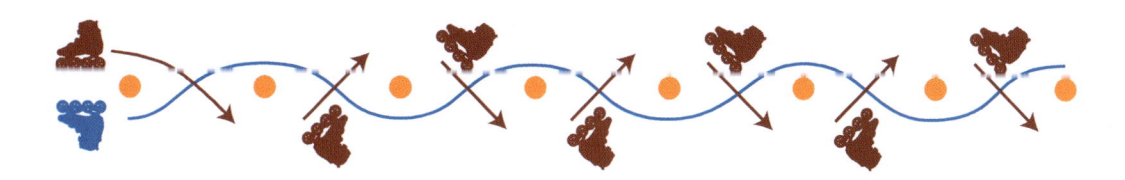

Troubleshooting of Common Problems

Swinging foot always facing backward and never forward.
Follow posture tips above to help you to rotate your hips more to the side.

Lack of movement energy.
The swinging foot is probably almost always perpendicular to the cone line. The foot needs to be at an angle in order for its contact with the ground to generate any movement. The closer the angle to the cone line, the more difficult the stroke will be but the more movement will be generated, just like gears on a bike.

62 **The Art of Falling:** Freestyle Slalom Skating

MEGA

Mega is the ultimate skills workout on cones. It covers transitions in both directions, and includes weight transfers and some fairly technical footwork. The body coordination and rhythm will also serve you well for the entirety of your slalom skating.

Step by Step Approach to Learning It

- Draw a sideways facing V between cones 1 and 2, between 3 and 4 and so on. i.e. in every other space.
- Start in a sideways facing V shape, between cones 1 and 2.
- Do Nelson for two cones until arriving in the next V.
- Do Backward Nelson for two cones until arriving in the next V.
- Repeat!

Complementary Tricks

Previous tricks to have learned:
- Nelson
- Backward Nelson

Tricks you should consider next:
- Sun
- Mexican

Tricks it mixes well with:
- All foundation tricks

MEGA

Tips on Style and Flow

Notes on correct posture
Your hips may rotate as much as 180 degrees back and forth, so this trick is impossible to do if your torso is not reasonably upright, making it a great way to improve posture during both Nelson and Backward Nelson.

Where weight should be
Your weight will be on whichever foot is snaking at that time. This will switch every two cones.

What the centre of mass should be doing
The centre of mass will experience a very slight rhythmic up/down motion and move at constant speed. Usually there will be a slightly more significant up/down bounce just before the back cross.

How to create power and energy
- Increase the amplitude of the snaking foot. This will force more significant hip rotation and make every movement stronger and more powerful
- Increase length that the swinging foot spends in contact with the ground.

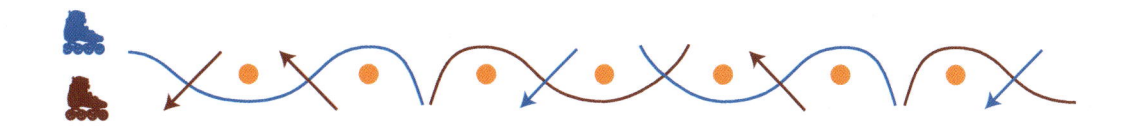

Troubleshooting of Common Problems

Keep forgetting to switch between Forward and Backward Nelsons.
Pause each time your feet are in a V shape facing sideways. Switch your weight from the foot it is on, to the other foot. Hey presto!

SUN

Sun simply involves transitioning from forward to backward and from backward to forward, in cones and while rotating in one continuous direction. Everything else about learning this trick is all about the specifics of which foot goes where, and then which edges and weight distributions create the best flow.

Step by Step Approach to Learning It

For rotating clockwise:

Cone 1: Crisscross, right foot leading.

Cone 2: Clockwise forward uncrossed heel pivot, using right heel.

Cone 3: Clockwise backward uncrossed heel pivot using left heel.

Cone 4: Back Cross, right foot leading.

Cone 5: Step around the left hand side of the cone as you step back to forward, picking up the right foot then the left foot.

Repeat!

Complementary Tricks

Previous tricks to have learned:
- Crisscross
- Backward Crisscross

Tricks you should consider next:
- Mega
- Volte

Tricks it mixes well with:
- Mega
- Forward/Backward Crisscross
- Forward/Backward Nelson

SUN

Tips on Style and Flow

Notes on correct posture
- Since you are rotating, having an upright torso is vital.
- A low centre of mass makes a huge difference too.
- Start with your arms out at the sides, and allow them to fall as you become more experienced with the trick.
- Check out the Spotting section (p 105). Hold the front cones in your sights until a moment before crossing the 4th cone.

Where weight should be
If rotating clockwise, your weight should always be on the skate that is on the left hand side of the cones as you move along. If rotating anti-clockwise, your weight should be on the skate that is on the right. Your skates will also always be edged away from the cone line.

What the centre of mass should be doing
You want to aim for the centre of mass to remain along the line of cones at a constant speed and height. This is especially challenging and important for cones 4 to 6.

How to create power and energy
Increase the amplitude of the wheel trace on the floor by lowering your centre of mass. Allow the feet to trace as far from from the cone line as possible around the area of 5th cone, while keeping the centre of mass over the line.

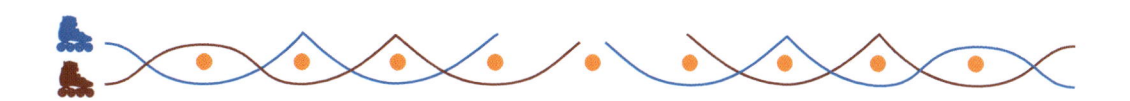

Troubleshooting of Common Problems

Cones 2 and 3.
You won't even know you're doing this one wrong. Check that your feet are each passing on different sides of cones. Each cone should be inside a pivot (see pivot section). Ensure that the pivoting wheel is next to a cone and that the wheels of both feet combine to make the shape of a pizza slice, with the cone in the middle, like a piece of pepperoni.

Interrupted flow during cones 5 and 6.
Your centre of mass is probably veering off to the side during cone 4, which means that you need to give yourself a push in order to come back over the cone line for cone 6. Keep leaning over the cone line during cone 4 and then 5 in order to get that flow.

PIVOTS: THE PARTICLE THEORY OF SKATING

Introducing the 24 Pivots 69

Troubleshooting 70

The Edge of the Satellite foot 73

The Most Valuable Pivots 74
    The Forward Uncrossed Heel Pivot
    The Backward Uncrossed Toe Pivot
    The Backward Crossed-Behind Toe Pivot ('Volte')

Using Pivots to solve problems and learn tricks 76
    Breaking tricks down into pivots

How to Use the Pivots 77
    Sun
    Crazy
    Mabrouk
    Screw
    Backward heel wheeling

PIVOTS: THE PARTICLE THEORY OF SKATING

When you look at a piece of art on a computer screen, TV screen or even in a newspaper, you might marvel at the beauty of the picture but know that if you look very close up that you will see a series of pixel dots which possess none of the beauty of the overall picture. Skating is very similar. If you take any slalom trick or combo and break it down and down and down, it is made up of a series of 'pivots' (or 'compasses'). A pivot is where one wheel remains in a fixed spot while the other foot traces a path around it. There are 24 basic pivots, and then even more when you start doing them with only one wheel on the outside foot too. These pivots can be developed on their own and away from slalom cones as a way of identifying and solving weak spots in your basic skills.

Sometimes the pivots are very easy to identify. For example in the tricks Sun, Brush or Crazy, the pivots used are very easy to spot, and are textbook pivots. In other tricks they are harder to spot, but still always there. In the Cockfoot/Chicken Leg where one foot does a tight circle or spin around a cone, it is a pivot without the central wheel being in contact with the ground, as with the Nelsons and 1-foot tricks. The Screw (cross-legged spin on only two wheels) is made up of two pivots, and having any issues with either of the pivots will render your Screw uncontrollable and unsustainable.

Introducing the 24 Pivots

There are 24 basic pivots, until you start removing more wheels from the ground:
- **Pivot wheel**: Heel/Toe (2 variables)
- **Direction**: Satellite foot travels forward/backward (2 variables)
- **Pivot types**: Uncrossed / Crossed-in-front / Crossed behind (3 variables)
- **Which foot or side**: Left foot/Right foot (2 variables)
- 2 x 2 x 3 x 2 = 24 pivots

Here they are in all their glory:
1. Forward Uncrossed Heel Pivot
2. Backward Uncrossed Heel Pivot
3. Forward Crossed-behind Heel Pivot
4. Backward Crossed-behind Heel Pivot
5. Forward Crossed-in-front Heel Pivot
6. Back Crossed-in-front Heel Pivot
7. Forward Uncrossed Toe Pivot
8. Backward Uncrossed Toe Pivot
9. Forward Crossed-behind Toe Pivot (Russian Volte)

10. Backward Crossed-behind Toe Pivot (Volte)
11. Forward Crossed-in-front Toe Pivot (J-turn)
12. Back Crossed-in-front Toe Pivot (Reverse J-turn)

13-24: As above, but on the other side, with the satellite foot becoming the pivot foot and vice versa.

There are 24 more if the 'satellite' foot is on the toe wheel, and 24 more on top of that if the satellite foot is on the heel wheel.

Troubleshooting

A pivot is just a simple mechanical process, which means that if you get any of the important things wrong, the pivot will not work.

Here is a checklist:
- The pivoting foot should be perpendicular to the centre of the satellite foot. Less than 90 degrees will result in the pivoting wheel moving around with the satellite foot, and more than 90 degrees will result in a side surf or inverted side surf movement.

Pivots - The Particle Theory of Skating   71

- The pivoting wheel must be on the correct edge. If it is on the incorrect edge then the pivot might move or your legs might splay apart into the splits.

pivot heel inside edge

pivot heel center edge

pivot heel outside edge

pivot toe inside edge

pivot toe center edge

pivot toe outside edge

72   **The Art of Falling:** Freestyle Slalom Skating

- Your weight must be on the satellite foot.

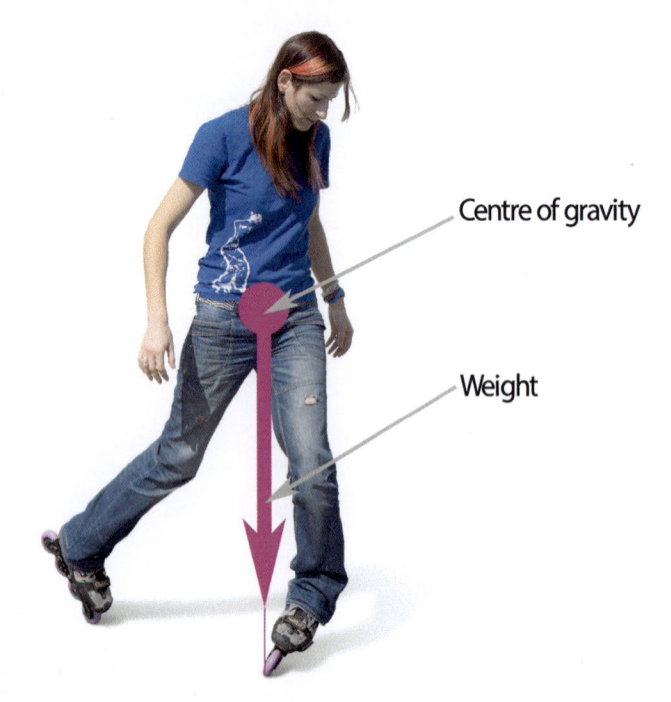

Centre of gravity

Weight

- Your upper body should generally be facing the direction of the pivot foot, i.e. in the direction that the toe is pointing.

Upper body faces the same direction as the toe of the pivoting foot

The Edge of the Satellite foot

Often when practising pivots the satellite foot will naturally be leaning in towards the pivot point. This makes sense from a stability point of view, but since freestyle is the art of continually falling from foot to foot you should also try the pivots with the satellite foot leaning away from the pivot.

In flowing freestyle, the pivots usually have the satellite foot leaning away from the pivot point.

74   *The Art of Falling:* Freestyle Slalom Skating

The Most Valuable Pivots

Clearly some of these 24 pivots are pretty awkward, and some are more useful than others. Here are the three MVPs of the pivot world. These pivots are the basic bread and butter of slalom:

The Forward Uncrossed Heel Pivot

- **Pivot wheel**: Heel
- **Pivot edge**: Outside edge
- **Direction**: Satellite foot moving forward
- **Pivot type**: 'Uncrossed' pivot
    1. Roll forward in a scissor position
    2. Put the front foot up onto the heel
    3. Allow the front foot to 'flop' onto its outside edge
    4. Keep looking at the front foot as the back foot now begins to circle around

Rolling forward before pivoting

The Backward Uncrossed Toe Pivot

- **Pivot wheel:** Toe
- **Pivot edge:** Outside edge
- **Direction:** Satellite foot moving backward
- **Pivot type:** 'Uncrossed' pivot
    1. Roll backward on both feet
    2. Extend a foot behind you (to lead), and roll it up onto the toe
    3. Allow the toe foot to 'flop' onto its outside edge
    4. Keep looking at the satellite foot as it begins to circle the toe

Tip: reach around with the toe-side arm and pull an imaginary string that is attached to the heel of the toe-foot. That will help it to flop onto the outside edge whilst also rotating the body correctly.

The Backward Crossed-Behind Toe Pivot ('Volte')

- **Pivot wheel:** Toe
- **Pivot edge:** Inside edge
- **Direction:** Satellite foot moving backward
- **Pivot type:** 'Crossed-behind' pivot
    1. Roll backward on both feet
    2. Extend a foot behind you (to lead), and roll it up onto the toe
    3. Allow the toe foot to 'flop' onto its inside edge
    4. Keep looking at the satellite foot as it begins to circle the toe

Rolling backward before pivoting

Tip: This is almost identical to the 'backward uncrossed toe pivot' (above) but the toe falls onto the other edge, resulting in the satellite foot rotating the other direction around the pivot toe.

Using Pivots to solve problems and learn tricks

Understanding the significance of pivots, and knowing how to use them for your own skating development will transform your skating. Unfortunately it takes a lot of experience to be able to identify how to use them for each trick, but once you have that deeper understanding and can work out which pivots are the basic building blocks of the tricks that you are learning, you will be able to not only solve your own skill problems as you learn, but also be able to accelerate your learning of the most high level wheeling tricks.

Breaking tricks down into pivots

As you will find out in the Style and Flow chapter (p 81), we generally have our weight on one foot or the other at any one time, and continuously fall back and forth between each foot. That is also how we change from pivot to pivot to pivot – our weight falls from foot to foot to foot. This enables us to get an initial idea of how many pivots make up each trick. It also tells us that there must be an even number if it is a trick that repeats itself.

If there are clear weight transfers, take each of the components and follow these steps:

- Knowing which foot your weight should be on at any moment reduces the 24 pivots down to 12.
- Knowing the direction of the satellite foot, assuming it is on the ground, reduces it to 6.
- Is there a clear arc on the ground, or are you falling over the satellite foot in a particular direction? If so then you know which side of your satellite foot the pivot should be. It should also give you an idea as to whether there is a crossed pivot involved.
- Heel or toe? This is all about your hips and head because the pivot foot will always face the satellite if it is on a toe, and face away if it is on the heel. Since the upper body should always face the same direction as the pivot foot, it should give you a good idea as to whether it is a heel or toe pivot.

If there are no clear weight transfers, such as in a static spin, there are usually two pivots being completely mixed. Once you know this, it is usually simple to put one foot on a heel or toe, make it stationary, get the other foot on all 4 wheels, and call it a pivot – and then do the same again for the other side which gives you the second pivot. This is very useful for crossed leg spins.

How to Use the Pivots

Almost every problem that you have when slaloming can be solved by working on the component pivots. They get your head, shoulders, arms, hips and feet in the correct orientation. They also get your weight on the correct foot and if you have a foot in the air, then they make sure it is in the correct position.

Once you have identified the component pivots, you can easily find out which one(s) are causing the problem. You can also work on your upper body individually with each pivot. When you return to the trick, you should find that the problem is no longer there, or at least greatly reduced, and your whole body is more relaxed and comfortably aligned than before.

Let us work through some examples, becoming gradually more difficult:

Sun

This is a very simple case and you can probably see and feel the pivots just by watching or doing it. Do it now.

How many weight transfers were there? Yes! There were 4! Correct! So before we have even looked for pivots, we know there are 4 to find.

Starting on the 2nd cone, we have a simple forward uncrossed heel pivot (p 74), then backward uncrossed heel pivot. These two are found almost every time we transition from forward to backward when skating normally. Then we have a Volte pivot (the backward crossed-behind toe pivot described on p 75) followed by the Russian Volte (forward crossed-behind toe pivot) and then back to the forward uncrossed heel pivot and so on.

The Volte is the most common problem in Sun, although you might also experience problems with first two pivots mainly concerning the edge of the pivoting heel. If the heels are on the inside edge for these pivots, then the legs splay apart and you risk doing the splits. It comes from not yet being comfortable with the rotary motion, but this problem can be easily solved by practising the pivots in the way described in the MVP 'Most Valuable Pivots' section (p 74).

Crazy

This is a slightly less easily broken down trick, but still pretty elementary. Do it and count the weight transfers and thus number of pivots.

There are again 4 pivots. Forward uncrossed heel pivot (p 74), backward uncrossed heel pivot, backward uncrossed toe pivot (p 75), forward uncrossed toe pivot. Try the Crazy again while feeling for these pivots. Make sure you try it away from cones too, as this is where movement is free enough to fully experience the pivots and weight transfers.

The reason that people find the Crazy difficult to learn is because the 3rd pivot, the backward uncrossed toe pivot, is particularly difficult to develop when it isn't removed from the context of a trick and learned as a pivot. The fall from the 3rd to 4th pivot is also much more difficult to learn in the context of the trick.

Mabrouk

The Mabrouk consists of the same movements and pivots as the Crazy. They were both based on the non-cones freestyle trick Grapevine. On the cones they look different though. A beginner slalomer will learn Mabrouk and have weight on both feet during the 'side surf' and 'inverted side surf' cones (cones 2 and 4). This will cause them to stall, experience a lot of friction and the need to push their way through the trick. If they understood and learned the pivots involved, they wouldn't suffer from any of those problems.

The pivots would also ensure that the hips and upper body were well orientated for the movements to happen with ease.

Screw

The Screw (sometimes known as the backward Korean Volte) is a great example of a trick which cannot easily be broken down into its component pivots. It is like being given a pancake and being told to find out the ingredients.

The pivots are the backward crossed-behind toe pivot (Volte, p 75), and the forward crossed-in-front toe pivot (J-turn).

Usually, someone will get comfortable on their two toe wheels and then learn Screw. Then the troubleshooting begins. One aspect of which will be their hips and upper body – very important components to get right when doing any spin. They will struggle for a long time, gradually gaining awareness of their hips, arms, shoulders, head, etc. Then they will learn to control them one by one. Finally they will be able to correct them all at once and they will be able to do a sustainable Screw.

By learning Screw as a combination of two pivots, it enables you to get your hips and upper body consistently correct while being on 5 wheels instead of 2 wheels. This affords you more time and brainpower to be directed towards getting these aspects correct and ingrained in your muscle memory. Then when you do the Screw for real the body will no longer be a problem.

Another troubleshooting aspect for Screw is the position of the feet and legs. Usually the legs are not crossed well because it is a pretty unnatural position to be in. It is usually the J-turn which is the weaker pivot and needs work. The ideal edges for Screw are inside edges for both toes. This is almost impossible unless you can do Butterfly (Screw position, but going in a straight line like a side-surf instead of a spin) however working on the Volte and J-turn pivots will help bring you away from extreme outside edges.

When you are trying to make the Screw travel along, usually you will find that one of your toes will facilitate you moving along the cones, and one will not. This is where you need to practise doing both pivots on only the toes. Surprisingly it is usually the Volte which is the problem here.

Backward heel wheeling

Surely this is beyond the limits of pivot theory. Surely pivot theory is useful for the more freestyle tricks, but is either non-existent or not useful for tricks such as a simple wheeling trick? Wrong! Happily the pivots are still very useful for even the most tedious and soul destroying of tricks.

There is very little going on in backward heel wheeling – balance seems to be the only thing. The wheel just goes along the cones and your job is to keep your skate up on the heel without falling backward. This is why the behaviour and orientation of the hips and upper body is especially important. The behaviour of the air leg, the orientation of the hips, the orientation of the shoulders and head are all covered if you develop your backward heel wheeling skills via pivots.

The two pivots are the backward crossed-behind toe pivot (Volte, p 75) and backward uncrossed heel pivot, but I recommend getting both of the pivot feet onto the toe wheel.

The two pivots will be easy for someone who is learning backward heel wheeling, so you would practise them with the satellite foot on the heel wheel. Once they are comfortable, it would be time to make sure all of the body is orientated correctly, and then start getting the weight back over to the satellite foot by introducing a slight bend to the satellite leg.

After working on these two pivots in this way and then gradually getting used to lifting the pivot toe, much of the frustration and progress-less practice sessions have been taken out of learning backward heel wheeling.

STYLE AND FLOW

What is Style?...83

Good Style = Technical Achievement...83

Elements..84
    Posture/Form
    Fluidity and Smoothness
    Power/Energy
    Whipping

STYLE AND FLOW

What is Style?

First off, let's be clear on what isn't meant by 'style' in this book, and that is personal-style. Style is a word used a good deal in the judging and evaluation of slalom skating, whilst being awarded totally different meanings by different people and in different contexts. Personal-style is something that attracts some whilst possibly putting off others – personal taste like clothing style, or music genre etc. Some like more aggressive style of slalom, others might like more elegant slalom, or perhaps fast and crazy slalom. The term 'style' in the context in which it is used in this book refers only to the quality of slalom, which is hopefully based on qualities which everyone can agree contributes towards good slalom – all the criteria other than 'did they execute the trick without knocking any cones?'.

Quality, beauty, and the feeling of flow for the observer. With poor style, it just looks like someone is just struggling through some technically difficult contortions through cones, whilst wearing skates, or at best, executing some very impressive skills. An observer might think 'Oh look, isn't that impressive', but not 'Wow, that's amazing' and almost never 'I want to do that'.

When someone is said to have good style, it suggests that they have a feeling of flow, ease, dignity and usually a certain amount of passion or engagement with what they are doing. It is truly inspiring to watch someone with these qualities.

You hear people talking about their favourite slalomers, and all around the world people's favourites are not the ones that they consider most technically able, but the ones that make what they do look easy and beautiful – the ones that inspire them. Sometimes a skater might be both – most technically advanced, and have top quality … and that's when you get skates named after you ….

Good Style = Technical Achievement

If the quality of your slalom is poor it not only affects the visual aspect of your slalom, but also the technical level.

If the fluidity is poor, the high levels of friction will prevent you from executing tricks which rely on momentum to carry them through, and if your feet never stray far from the cones (low 'amplitude') or if your centre of gravity does not move smoothly, you will not be able to maintain the energy to keep some tricks going. The most important style aspect however, for the achievement of technical tricks, is posture and form – this can make or break your success in a trick.

Dismiss the importance of 'quality and style' at your peril, for you will not be able to control yourself well on your skates without it.

Elements

There must be a million ways to define style and none of them is perfect or universal due to its being such an intangible concept. Here are some aspects of slalom quality that have been broken down and often related to simple physics. A cold hard approach to evaluating beauty, I grant you, but I'm afraid that it is what perceived beauty so often comes down to …

These 'elements' are not intended as any requirement or standard for slalom, but only to be used as a way of troubleshooting. If you want to achieve a smoother appearance, solve the problem of your unco-ordinated and frantic looking arms or improve your speed, you will need to understand the physical changes that need to take place. Be aware that any alterations to the quality of your slalom need to be made at the foundation level. Once your most basic tricks have a good style and quality it will automatically transfer to the higher level tricks.

Posture/Form

Easily recognised as an important part of style, posture and form is integral to enabling a skater to raise their technical level. So what is good posture and body form? And how would you go about correcting it?

Unhelpful body position

Well-balanced body position

Torso position

The torso should usually be upright. The only really practical way of evaluating what your torso is doing is to take a video of your skating and watch for the angle of your torso as you slalom. You might notice yourself bowing over more when you do something which makes you feel off balance. It might feel like it should help, but it is actually detrimental to your balance.

Having an upright torso becomes most important when you are doing any kind of rotation – having your body in a giant Z shape means that more of your body mass is further from the central axis of rotation. This in turn causes any imperfections in your spin to be exaggerated, and leads to your loss of balance.

To correct this, start with a very simple backward slalom technique such as Back Cross, since it's when we are looking over our shoulder at the cones ahead of us that we are most tempted to bow over. When you are performing this trick, and looking behind you, you should feel as if you are leaning back, and thrusting your hips out in front of you. You should also feel as if you are sticking your chest out a little too much.

When you are comfortable with that, try it with a rotating trick such as the Sun, Italian, or Mexican, or just switching between Forward and Back Cross at your leisure. If you are already working on more advanced tricks such as the Swan, Screw or Korean Volte then have a go at those, reminding yourself all the time that although getting your torso upright feels very unstable right now, it will result in greatly increased stability and comfort later.

When eliminating a bad habit you need to change, and change is hard with tough times coming before the eventual improvement. Postural changes are the most painful changes to make, and of the postural changes, the torso is possibly that most difficult.

Hips

The hips should be rotated and tucked underneath the torso. Having your backside sticking out makes you look uncomfortable, but it also throws off your balance for the reasons stated above.

If you see in a video of yourself that your backside is indeed sticking out, and you don't find it easy to rotate your hips to tuck them underneath your torso, then I recommend attending a Tai Chi class. That should sort it out, along with enabling you to lower your centre of gravity too, bringing us to the next point, centre of gravity:

Centre of Gravity

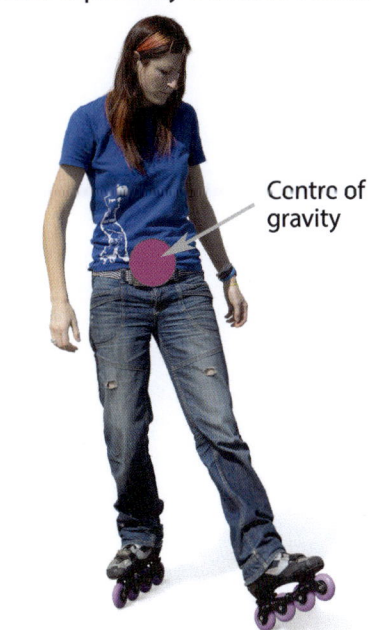

The centre of gravity should be kept low, as if sitting down. This is more of a means to an end, enabling all of the other postural and style elements to fall into place. Your centre of gravity is usually between navel and pelvis and always wants to be along your central axis.

Keeping your centre of gravity low enables you to bend and straighten your knees to a much greater degree, which does a number of things:
- Your legs will act as a buffer to keep your body more steady and 'floaty.'
- Your feet will have a much larger range of movement, enabling you to achieve more 'contorted' looking tricks.
- Your feet will have a much larger area of movement, giving your skating a much more powerful appearance.
- Your speed can be regulated more easily, to iron out stopping and starting.

Keeping your centre of gravity along the line of your central axis keeps you in greater control and more able to take larger forces without buckling or bending over, enabling you to use more power in your skating.

Arms

Arms are a giveaway of any discomfort or lack of confidence in a skater's slalom and are invaluable tools to help maintain balance.

When looking at videos it can be hard to tell exactly what your arms should be doing. You may look at someone skating, and decide that they are out of control because their arms are flying around the place, and then see a video of a very highly regarded skater, looking beautiful and energetic, and notice that their arms are also flying about in an uncontrolled fashion, but somehow looking good and not as if the skater has a lack of control. Conversely the same is true for having arms that are doing little - one person might have quite motionless arms and look ultra relaxed as a result, but someone else might be keeping their arms subdued, and look very stiff and awkward as a result. What to do?

The key is in the relaxation. If arms are tense then they are not useful as balancing devices – they cannot react to the movements of the body and help keep everything in balance. You can tell your arms what to do to balance a move, but this only works to a small degree – they need to be able to react in a relaxed manner to your body's movement.

Conversely, if your arms are totally limp, they are equally useless as balancing devices and you might as well not have them. Your arm muscles need to be able to tense and relax in response to the needs of the moment. Watch a video of a high level but very animated skater, and you will see that the arms move in very strong and sudden movements, but all in a relaxed way.

Correcting the arms is actually quite enjoyable and simple, but requires a fair amount of patience. You need to start with basics, as with all of the other style corrections, and do all of your tricks with the arms totally limp (yes, useless limp). If you relax your arms totally, they should feel like annoying dead weights hanging off your shoulders. Only when you are able to perform your more basic tricks and transitions with zero reliance on your arms will you be finally rid of any bad habits and residual tension in your arms and shoulders.

When you are doing this, you will need to give your arms and shoulders a good shake down before entering the cones each time and, as you are going through the cones, you'll notice your arms starting to slip back into bad habits (a classic one is an elbow behaving as if a puppeteer is tugging it upwards) – catch this as soon as you can by shaking out your arms and shoulders again while you are skating to bring them back to total limpness again.

When you have spent a while doing this, enjoy some of your usual slalom again, and you should notice that your arms feel a lot more spontaneous and in tune with the movements of your body and skating.

Head

The head is an interesting subject. The two main concerns that people have are the two things that I'm very liberal about. One is head tilt – some very good and elegant skaters choose to tilt their head downwards to quite a degree, and some keep it as upright at possible. The other is whether or not you should be looking at the cones or not – of course you should! If you can do any of your tricks without looking at the cones, then good on you, but no need!

The important issue with your head is the direction in which you are looking. For maximum smoothness in your skating, it should keep as much to one direction as possible, and usually this means mainly looking in the overall direction in which you are travelling.

Looking in the direction of travel

If you are rotating, then spotting is important. Not only to avoid getting dizzy, but also to help the speed and ease of your rotations. When spotting, you should look at whatever cone is convenient, and allow your body to rotate as much as you are able to, without moving the head. When you are twisted to the max, allow your head to flick around 360 degrees, and lock your eyes on the next cone, and your body can continue the rotation.

As with altering the angle of your torso, changing the behaviour of your head, or rather, where you are looking, is a challenging process where you will need to take a large step backward in order to make the eventual improvement. But rest assured that it's worth it!

Fluidity and Smoothness

Flow is made up of two elements: fluidity and smoothness.

Fluidity

The term 'fluidity' in this book refers to the ease of movement that a skater has when skating. It is the difference between the appearance of skating through a thick liquid, or skating through a thin liquid. When some skaters slalom they look as if there is no friction slowing their skates down – they appear to trickle through the cones with speed and ease.

When a skater who is lacking in fluidity skates, it will look as if a lot of physical effort is being put into pushing their way through and around the cones. This is what we want to avoid – the stickiness and effort.

In any type of skating, with speed skating being the perfect example, fluidity can be achieved in the exactly the same way:

- The skater's weight must usually be either on one foot or the other, and not shared between the two feet. There are exceptions to this rule (for tricks such as Crisscross) but for almost all other tricks, maximum fluidity can only occur if weight is switching from foot to foot as if in a relay.
- When the weight switches from one foot to the other, it must be as a result of the centre of gravity falling. You must fall from one foot to the other. I don't believe that there are any exceptions to this rule.

> *Skating is the art of continually toppling from one foot to the other, and freestyle skating is no exception – it is what creates the beauty of the movements, and the 'leg bending' appearance of some of them.*

Improving your fluidity can be difficult if you have focused on tricks of a higher technical level before getting a good quality base level, but there is one exercise that is really worth the effort, and is perfect for those who have not played around much with the basics much before moving on:

- Pass through the cones, switching as often as you choose, between forward Crisscross and backward Crisscross. Try to turn so that your head is always able to stay in one direction, and try to get through the cones as fast as you can. This is a fairly easy exercise for most people and so you should remember whilst you are doing it that the end-goal is to do it as fast as possible – you should find that over time, you spend less and less time with weight on both feet, and there is a lot more feeling of falling from one foot to the other during transitions.

Make sure that you are doing both your comfortable and less comfortable sides, and also start using some forward and Back Snake in there too.

To then use your head to assist with improving your fluidity, always make sure when you switch between backward and forward, that you always turn clockwise, or always turn counter-clockwise. This will force you to practise keeping your head always facing the direction in which you are travelling in order to minimise hesitation during transitions.

Smoothness (floating appearance)

The term 'smoothness' in this book refers to the extent to which a skater appears to 'float' during freestyle tricks. The term 'float' might seem a bit extreme, however this is exactly how a skater will appear if one simple physical rule is obeyed:

> *If a skater's centre of gravity moves along at a constant velocity (constant speed, constant direction), then the skater literally appears to be floating, no matter what the feet are doing.*

The reason that this effect is achieved is because if the centre of gravity travels along the cones or ground in this way, there is no change in momentum of the skater, and so no external/additional forces are needed – thus the skater becomes a simple mass in motion, like an orbiting planet.

Most skaters don't give much thought to what their centre of gravity is up to and focus instead on what their limbs are doing, however although this might result in smooth transitions at skate level (i.e. smooth transition of weight from one foot to the other), it doesn't give the skater that look of surreal hovering which results from the centre of gravity remaining steady.

There are various ways to train your body to keep your centre of gravity steady:

Linear direction

Try some of your tricks whilst keeping the centre of gravity travelling at the same rate along the cones – iron out the faster and slower parts to those tricks by slowing everything down to the speed of the slowest part. Also try switching between forward and backward basics, but always keeping your body moving at a constant rate.

Your body and feet must just behave like a cradle whose job it is to transport the centre of gravity along at a constant velocity.

Up and down direction

By keeping your centre of gravity lower, you are more able to keep it at the same height all the way along the line of cones when doing slalom. Having a higher centre of gravity strips you of your ability to stabilise its movement.

Side to side direction

If your centre of gravity deviates from the central line of the slalom cones, you will need a force to bring it back over the cones again, usually in the form of a push.

A classic case is the trick 'Crazy'. If you're finding that you can't stop yourself going backward, or don't seem to have the strength to 'push' yourself back over the cones, then clearly something is wrong. We don't want to stop any movement in this move, or do any pushing whatsoever. If you watch someone who is comfortable with the Crazy, you will see that their centre of gravity remains over the cones, and it is only their feet that swing backward and forward across the cones like a pendulum.

Leaning over the cones in the Crazy

Style and Flow   91

Another great example where keeping the centre of gravity along the line of cones is of utmost importance, is the Sun. Many people allow their body to drift out to the side of the cones when switching from backward to forward. Their feet come out to the side of the cones, and so they allow their body to follow. No! Your centre should remain over the cones. If you try this, you will feel the difference.

Leaning over the cones in the Sun

Sometimes, you might choose to deliberately sacrifice some of your smoothness. Perhaps you want to do a huge sweeping Volte, or do something a bit more deliberately bouncy and dancey. Smoothness as described here is just an ingredient which can be used to season your freestyle to fit your own style, taste and mood.

Power/Energy

This is often the inspirational quality of a freestyle skater. A skater who has plenty of power and energy in their skating usually appears to have limitless confidence and sure-footedness in the movements that they make, using large forces and plenty of enthusiasm. It is almost as if they have no concern for the cones which lie under their body – they perform tricks with an appearance of wanton abandon.

It is these skaters who are able to push their freestyle to the limits of musical expression and the expression of pretty much anything. The strong and bold movements are also captivating to watch – the avoidance of cones is no longer the most impressive feat for an observer, it is instead the mesmerising sweeping movements of the feet and body.

Amplitude using back cross

There are several factors at play. Here are a few of them, together with some accompanying exercises:

Amplitude

If you use as much of the area around the cones as possible, making your movements as wide as you can, they will increase in strength, power and beauty. As a convenient side effect you'll also find that you're knocking fewer cones.

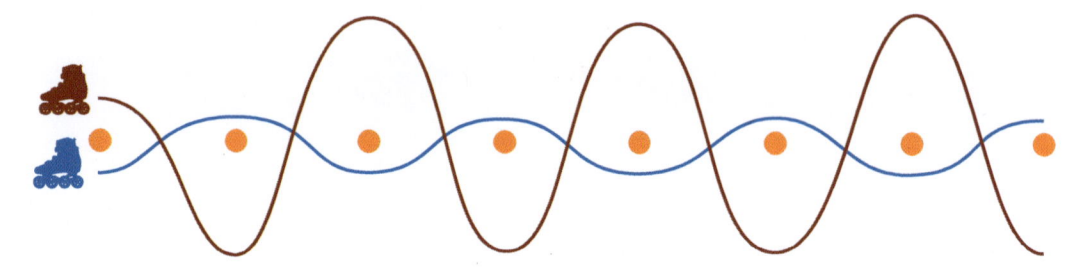

A good place to start is with Back Snake – a much-neglected move of great beauty when done well. When you are doing the Back Snake, get your feet to make as wide and bendy Snake as possible on the ground, really wide, exaggerated and curvaceous. After that go for the Nelsons, which are part Snake anyway, and then have a go with your other tricks.

A really good visualisation is to imagine that there are two light beams running parallel to the cones, about 30cm away from the line each side. Each time your foot breaks the beam of light a buzzer goes off (in your imagination). See how much you can make the buzzer whine. It's a good idea to actually draw a line each side of the cones to aim for. Perhaps one day I'll own a state-of-the-art training facility where we can actually set up a real light gate and buzzer, so my students won't have to listen to my terrible buzzer impersonations anymore.

Centre of Gravity

It's the centre of gravity again, but with a difference! I will now go against what I advised during the section above on smoothness. As discussed there, it's all about personal choice and taste, and floating down the cones isn't what some skaters aspire to do. It's a great exercise for stabilising yourself, and improving the quality and control of your movements, but I would only want to float down the cones if I was skating to classical music or a very bland love song – which I very rarely do.

When working on power and energy in your slalom, you might want to throw your centre of gravity around a bit. I tend to bounce it slightly when doing more dance type moves, but you might want to consider throwing it out to the side sometimes. It is very difficult to describe what I mean here, so I will refer to a few tricks which you may or may not know. The Seatbelt, the Reaching Back Snake, and the 3-or-More Cone Volte all involve throwing the centre of gravity out to the side of the line of cones, very briefly, before allowing it to fall back in again. If any of these tricks are done without throwing the centre of gravity around, then they look like weak impersonations of the tricks.

Arms and upper body

These are very important to power and energy when doing any kind of activity. During freestyle skating they need to twist and counterbalance in a way to assist the amplitude of the move itself.

The best method to get your arms and upper body operating in a way which is complimentary to your slalom tricks is to go right back to the basics such as Swinging Basketweave and Nelson and get your arms working in opposition to your leg and foot movement, just like when you're walking and running. When your arms have recovered from the usually awkward beginnings they will really get into the swing of things, and you will find yourself able to increase the amplitude and force used in your slalom tricks by increasing the swing and power in your arms. When your whole body is working together in a trick it really does feel great.

Direction changing

Maintaining power in your changes of direction, particularly when at the end of a line of cones, is very important to the overall energy in a combo.

When you change direction, you have momentum travelling in one direction, which needs to be changed to be going in the other direction. This requires a force to push you back, and as already discussed in the fluidity section, we like to use the force of gravity! You want to fall back along the line of cones. If you keep your centre of gravity over your feet all the way until the end of the cones, you will find yourself in a rather precarious position where if you stop your feet, you will just fall over, since your body will just keep on travelling. So, many people prefer to slow down as they approach the end of the cones.

Instead of slowing down, try to stop your centre of gravity half a cone early whilst letting your feet carry on until the end of the cones, before quickly returning to where your centre of gravity is before you fall over. You will need to have your centre of gravity very low in order for this to work well. This is a great way to change direction without using any pushing at all.

A great exercise for this is 4-cone slalom. It's great for improving most of the power and energy factors in your slalom. Set up 4 or 5 cones at 80cm spacing, and just go for it. No plan, no nothing, just slalom on them. After the initial awkwardness of not having anything planned, you will find it quite liberating and will begin to enjoy the mess and chaos of nothing fitting perfectly into the 4 cone run. When you have got to that stage, start trying to speed up everything you are doing. You will find that you really need to keep your centre of gravity around the middle few cones and will need to increase the amplitude of everything that you do with your feet. The sound that your wheels make on the floor will get louder and everything will start to feel more powerful.

Another exercise for direction changing is backward snaking continuously up and down a line of about 6 cones (make it an even number). At the start you will find yourself unable to keep the Snake going continuously during the change of direction, but as you fall more and more towards the direction in which you want to go, the Snake will lose less and less speed, and no extra pushes will be necessary.

Whipping

This is that explosive moment when a skater's feet seem to go **KaBAM!** for a split second before normal service is resumed. It can be caused by the upper body winding itself up like an elastic band before quickly unwinding as the legs flick around to catch up, however is it usually caused by an extreme backward outside edge. Examples of tricks that whip well are 'Mexican, Italian, Curly Link, Ride and even Mabrouk sometimes. A good mental image is someone starting a chain saw.

To try out the feel of the whip, practise your backward uncrossed toe pivot (see the Pivots chapter, p 67) but initiate it by keeping your pivot foot on all 4 wheels and doing a Crisscross before entering the pivot. The trailing foot (soon to become the satellite foot) should trace an almost straight path because it has all of the weight on it, while the leading foot should make a very extremely exaggerated and tight 'C' shape on an extreme outside edge, free of any burden of weight. Over time this will become bigger, stronger and faster until it accelerates you into barely controlled rotary motion.

SKILLS AND DRILLS

Skill: One-foot balance and control *99*
    Drill 1: Skating on one foot
    Drill 2: 3-turns

Skill: Edge control *101*
    Drill 1: Alternating between edges during toe and heel rolls
    Drill 2: Pivots

Skill: Rotary motion *102*
    Drill: Pivots

Skill: Falling *103*
    Drill 1: The Gingerbread Man.
    Drill 2: Toppling from pivot to pivot.

Skill: Spotting *105*
    Drill: Learning to spot

SKILLS AND DRILLS

There are many skills that can be developed to help with the learning and improvement of slalom. Here are some of the most useful:

Skill: One-foot balance and control

Since all of our weight is almost always on one foot or the other at any one time, we need to be able to comfortably balance on each foot no matter which direction it is going or which edge it is on. We are unable to have our weight in the correct place if we need to split it between our two points of ground contact. We also need to be able to switch our feet between forward and backward whilst keeping the weight on one foot.

Drill 1: Skating on one foot

If you are not yet able to propel yourself along on only one foot, roll forward in the scissor position, with the back foot on the toe. Now try meandering the front foot from side to side. Eventually you will be able to pick up the back toe. This drill is a whole lot easier when your wheels are rockered.

Once you are able to go forward, try going backward. Your feet will be in the same configuration, but this time your toe wheel will be leading the way even though it is behind you.

Drill 2: 3-turns

'3-turns' from artistic skating are a great way to learn to switch your feet between forward and backward whilst keeping your weight on that foot. There are eight basic 3-turns (forward to backward/backward to forward, clockwise/counter-clockwise, left foot/right foot) and they are so called because the foot traces the figure '3' on the ground. There are plenty of videos on the internet, but attending an artistic skating class specifically to learn these would be a pretty good idea even if you have to be the inline skate and jeans-wearing weirdo – I speak from experience.

3-turns begin on one edge and end up on the other edge after the switch. In slalom we also use rockers (outside edge to outside edge), counters (inside edge to inside edge) and what I call 'swivels' where we use a centre edge and swivel on the middle two wheels.

Skill: Edge control

Skating with our skates on the correct edge means the difference between free flowing movement and grinding to a halt. You need to be at home on either edge whilst going forward or backward. You also need to be able to feel which edge you are on and get your skates on an edge without having to look down and check. If you find it hard to get a particular edge then there are two usual reasons – either you simply lack the control as yet, or your skates don't suit your body mechanics. Neither of these is a problem because the first can be solved using these drills, and the second can be solved by adjusting the alignment of your frame in relation to your skates. If your frames are not adjustable then you might want to consider getting some skates with adjustable frames.

Drill 1: Alternating between edges during toe and heel rolls

Roll forward in a scissor position and put the back foot up onto the toe.
Roll forward in a scissor position and put the front foot up onto the heel.
For each of these wheel-rolls, allow the foot that has all four wheels on the ground to flop from side to side, from edge to edge. Gradually extend the time that you spend on each edge.
Repeat this on the other foot and also whilst going backward.

Drill 2: Pivots

Practising the pivots (see the Pivots chapter, p 67) whilst varying the edge on the satellite foot is challenging if your edge control is weak. However, it is very useful since it is pivots which make up the tricks that you are learning in slalom. Typically the satellite foot needs to lean away from the pivot point in order to maintain flow in slalom. Pivots also enable you to improve your control of the edge on the pivot wheel.

Skill: Rotary motion

One of the most common problems during slalom tricks which have a rotation element is the upper body not joining in the party. The feet can do everything necessary to make a trick work but if the upper body doesn't rotate along with the feet then it isn't going to end happily. Similarly if the upper body gets thrown into a rotation too much, then the rotation won't last very long because the upper body will flick back like an unwinding elastic band. Once this skill is developed, it may need re-developing for every new type of rotating trick.

Drill: Pivots

Any trick that you are using will have pivots associated with it. Go and work on those pivots and don't be content with a 180-degree rotation. Go for at least 360 degrees or more. If you are unable to achieve a complete rotation with any pivot then take a look at the behaviour of your upper body. Your entire body, including legs and arms should be absolutely frozen during a pivot. Any movement of the upper body to encourage rotation is poison to you – it may help you to rotate further but it is also concealing your lack of skill in this area and not assisting its development.

# Skill: Falling

Skating in its entirety is all about falling – falling from foot to foot or even falling well and creatively through the air when doing a trick in aggressive skating. Falling is king. A great way to develop the falling sensation for yourself is a little exercise that works wonders for getting kids and beginners able to start skating in the first place. It's called the Gingerbread Man.

Drill 1: The Gingerbread Man.

Stand in a stick-man position, as if you're stuck on the door to the men's room, or alternatively lying on a baking tray with other freshly made gingerbread man cookies. Now, everyone knows that if any of your joints move then you are going to break and little crumbs of gingerbread are going to fall to the floor – an unpleasant scenario that you'll want to avoid. Whilst maintaining your rigid shape, start toppling from side to side with your feet parallel – if your feet are in a V position then you'll start skating forward. You should try to recreate this toppling feeling every time you skate, whether it's freestyle or in a straight line.

104 The Art of Falling: Freestyle Slalom Skating

Drill 2: Toppling from pivot to pivot.

You can also work the falling skill by toppling to and from different pivots (without cones) as this is exactly what we do in slalom. Try to hold each pivot as long as possible before eventually toppling into another pivot – your satellite foot will need to be leaning away from the pivot point to facilitate the toppling. When you topple into the next pivot you should find that you have fresh motion from the falling motion of your centre of gravity.

Skill: Spotting

Spotting is the art of rotating your body whilst keeping your head facing one direction. It is great for reducing dizziness when on or off cones, however when doing slalom it also enables your speed and smoothness to increase considerably. By steadying the head your point of view remains the same, reducing the time lag that you get when your mind adjusts to its new view of the cones as your head moves gradually around. A constant head position also keeps your upper body more steady, giving you a smoother flow through the cones.

Drill: Learning to spot

Start by just standing in one spot and looking at something on the wall. Slowly turn your feet until you feel that you cannot go any further without taking your eyes off your focal point. It will be up to about 180 degrees. Then keep your feet where they are and flick your head around to look at your focal point again before allowing the feet to once again continue around to face the same way as your head. This is typical 'spotting' which is done by dancers. In slalom it is ever so slightly different – if we did this then we would have cones flying everywhere. In slalom we look down. So put a cone on the ground, say 40cm away from your feet, and repeat the above exercise whilst looking at the cone instead of a point on the wall. You will find that you can turn a lot more before your head needs to flick around, making it easier.

PRACTISE PRACTISE PRACTISE

Practice Exercises 110
    Slow motion
    Visualisation
    Knee-bend exercise
    Technique intervals
    Off Cones Freestyle
    3 times per move

Organising Practice 116

Monthly Projects and Themes 118

Getting Frustrated? 119

PRACTISE PRACTISE PRACTISE

It is said that to break into the realm of excellence at any endeavour, you need ten thousand hours of practice and at least ten years. In slalom there are not yet so many participants that you need this number of hours and years in order to become world class, though these figures give us an appreciation of just how much practice gets done by those that excel in their sport.

You must practise enough …

Practising once a week is fine so long as you aren't planning to become internationally successful and will not feel hard done by when others learn much faster. It all comes down to practice – no one is born a good skater. I consider that I cannot spin and that I am terrible at wheeling so I'll never be very successful at doing 7s (a one-wheel travelling spin) but the reality is that I just don't enjoy those parts of skating and so practise them very little. I also use my age as an excuse when I see teenagers picking up the wheeling tricks much faster than I do nowadays, but that's also not fair because younger people will often spend hours and hours absorbed in practice every day while I am busy writing some book about it instead.

… but don't over do it

Be wary of practising for too long at one time and not taking enough rest between practice sessions – your neural pathways need to repair and strengthen just as your muscles do. It is also easy to forget that your body is actually doing physical exercise while you practise. I was once doing up to fifty hours a week alongside a full time desk job for the two months before my first competition back in 2003. Two weeks before the big weekend I had to almost stop skating because my legs had all but given up working and I could hardly even drag myself up a flight of stairs. It hadn't occurred to me that I should be behaving like an athlete by modifying my diet and providing my body with increased amounts of rest and nutrition. I feasted for two weeks on huge amounts of protein and carbs, cut out alcohol and since I couldn't skate I was also getting to bed earlier and not getting up for pre-work practice sessions. I have never made that mistake again but often come across those that have. It is very easy to forget that we are athletes!

The optimal amount of practice

It is difficult to sustain a good quality of practice if you go over twenty hours a week, so working with three hours a day for six days a week with one rest day is ideal for maximising your learning. I also recommend splitting it up into two sessions per day if you can as little and often is highly effective when developing skills. If you are going to practise this much then you must make sure you eat, sleep and stretch to support your the physical work that your body is doing.

Practice Exercises

You should feel free to just run through all of your tricks and work on them in any way you choose, however if you want to accelerate your learning or even just provide some added variety to your practice, try these exercises:

Slow motion

When trying to improve the smoothness of a trick or a combo, it can sometimes be like polishing a brick using a piece of fine cloth – you need to unearth the core problems that you have with that move, or transitions within that combo, and then iron them out.

A great way of doing this is taking the move or combo, and seeing how slowly you can do it. Whatever speed you begin with, you must continue that speed – no speeding up and slowing down as you're going along – concentrate on keeping the centre of gravity floating along with constant height and direction as you travel down the line of cones. Or, if you are reversing your direction during a combo, that the centre of gravity gradually stops going in one direction and starts in the opposite direction – no sudden changes.

If you do this exercise correctly it will be incredibly difficult and require a lot of your muscles since you'll need to balance on each foot a little longer than usual, before allowing yourself a controlled fall onto the other foot each time.

It should feel as if you are doing Tai Chi

As you travel down the line you should notice times when it feels impossible to do it slowly – that there are parts that need to be quickly skipped over. These are the problems. Keep going over these bits, gradually slowing them down further and further and you should find that with a lot of concentration and effort you can do it. It's a bit like when you have found a knot in a muscle and are slowly working it out. These problem areas of 'non smoothness' are usually caused by insufficient foundations, such as discomfort with going backward on the outside edge of your bad foot - this slow motion exercise exposes these deficiencies and allows you to work on them whilst remaining in the context of the move that you are developing.

When you again perform the move or combo at your normal speed, you should notice a strong improvement, so long as you really did work through the problem areas several times. This exercise is also a great way to warm up when practising a competition combo – throwing yourself right into your combo is a really bad plan, particularly at the earlier stages – it can throw you off, and reinforce past mistakes in both technical and style areas, setting you up for a miserable session. If you begin by running through your combo in slow motion (I often put a piece of slow music on my headphones) it reminds your body of what is expected, reinforcing all the positive habits instead of the negative ones.

This slow motion exercise can be used for changing pretty much all aspects of your slalom, including adjusting your arms, head, weight transfer etc, whereas rushing through moves allows you to 'cover up' problems, and results in chaotic looking slalom - genuine chaos, not the 'fun and impassioned slalom' kind.

Visualisation

This is used in most physical activities that I can think of. Whether it is for psychological or technical enhancements, it works wonders. I found that boring meetings were the best times for inventing new moves and combos – rather than while skating. In your mind you can do all kinds of amazing and barely possible things, and time and time again, weeks, months or years later, I have found myself doing those things that I once daydreamed about. But! This is about its relevance to practice ….

When you're physically on the slalom line doing the move, it can be hard to implement the changes that you are trying to do. Whether it is to get a bit more rotation during the Italian or Mabrouk, keep your knee up during heel wheeling, or put a bit more weight on the other toe when doing the Screw, visualisation can often be an excellent tool.

Imagining yourself doing everything correctly, and mentally correcting yourself as you go, is great. It keeps you away from the failure, away from falling, and allows you to sort it all out without the pressure of also having to be balancing at the same time. Visualisation is commonly used for sports where someone is in the air and can't really stop and think for a moment halfway through a somersault – just like we can't really stop and think easily during some of our moves.

It's useful for changing the way that you use your head, relaxing your arms, becoming familiar with the feeling of sinking into the Swan instead of straightening up into it – the list is endless. During practice of a difficult move, make sure you visualise successfully doing the move before each and every attempt. It will reinforce your intended improvements, whilst purging your mind of any bad habits which might linger from the previous attempt.

Knee-bend exercise

Not enough knee bend is not actually the problem that needs solving here. 'Bend your knees more!' is rarely what any kind of instructor actually means. It might possibly be what they think they mean, or they might be consciously saying it to get what they want, but rarely is it what they need someone to do. What they actually want is for that person to use their knees more. Rigidly bent knees are little more use than straight ones, except that it does allow a much greater rotation of the feet with respect to the hips.

So, we want the torso and hips to feel a little more like a mass on a spring. We want the centre of gravity to be insulated from all the nasty goings on which are happening at ground level, which might give it cause to stop and start, or suffer some other kind of disturbance which will jog the eye of the entranced beholder. During most slalom moves there are times where you feel you have plenty of 'push', and others where you find yourself stuck, trying to budge your feet along, unsure of where you're supposed to get the energy to continue on to link up with the 'plenty of push' part of the move.

Here is an analogy from my physics class: We use electricity mainly during the day, and much less at night. Power stations however, do not switch on/off or increase/reduce their production based on the time of day – it just doesn't work like that – instead, they work constantly around the clock. There is excess energy sometimes and a deficiency at other times. So what happens? The excess energy is stored until it is needed to supplement a high demand, thus levelling it out. One of the methods to effect this is to use this energy to pump water uphill, where it is then stored as potential energy, ready to be released downhill at anytime.

This is exactly what we do in slalom. At times in a move with plenty of motion, we store the energy, and then when we are grinding to a halt and need to call on those reserves, we can release the energy to be used to get us through. We store the energy in our knees. When we bend the knees, we are storing energy, and when we straighten the knees we are using that energy and turning it into motion of some kind. Good examples are watching someone jump – bending the knees before takeoff, and also some speed skating – you can see the straightening of the knee when the skater is trying to get everything they can out of the leg.

So, during slalom our knees need to be bending and straightening like pistons, working all the time. Unfortunately however, if you were to be told when to bend your knees and when to straighten them, you'd become a total overthinking mess, with horrible slalom – it's best not to bother the conscious mind. Instead try the following exercise which gives the body an opportunity to learn directly the benefits of bending its knees at certain points.

The exercise:

1. Do your move with knees too bent. Far too bent. So bent that you can only just barely make it through the move. Make sure your quads are burning and you're exhausted at the end, and also make sure you looked completely

stupid. Anything less and you were not bending them enough for this exercise.
2. Now repeat but with legs completely straight (if you're worried about your joints, don't lock them straight).
3. Repeat steps 1 and 2 as many times as you like, making sure that you finish with a step 1.
4. Relax and try the move normally again, and you should feel the difference.

Technique intervals

Technique intervals are used in speed skating which is where I first picked up the concept, and so I have kept the term for the application to slalom. Really it should be called 'focus-based practice' or something more descriptive, but I'm already used to the speed skating term.

When we are learning a skill, there is usually a lot to think about. I think I was about 10 when I was learning to ride a horse over jumps – there was so much to think about all at once! Do this with your hands, do this with your knees, this with your feet, this with your head, this with your body … I never seemed to get them all at once, and it resulted in me feeling frustrated, idiotic, and totally inadequate. Exactly the same goes for slalom. I learned very early on that standing there, giving improvement after improvement to someone when they are trying to learn a move is possibly the most destructive thing that you can do to their motivation, as they have no focus, and it sets them up to fail.

A much better solution is to isolate each single improvement and focus on them one at a time. I also recommend only working on two or three improvements during any one day. Here is how I suggest using technique intervals on a slalom move or combo:

1. Choose two or three different 'focuses' (let's say having weight only on one foot at a time and not bending over forward into a Z shape).
2. Do the move/combo, focusing solely on the 1st focus. In this example, think about little other than making sure that you have your weight only on one foot or the other. Your move will suffer as a result. You might find yourself bending over, you might find yourself all over the place. Don't worry about it. Go all out to make sure you are falling from one foot to the other for the entire run.
3. Do the move/combo again, but focusing solely on the 2nd focus. In this example, only think about sticking your chest out, feeling your spine in relaxed vertical alignment, and tucking your hips under your torso. Again your move might suffer, particularly your other focus(es), but don't worry.
4. If you have a 3rd focus, do that now
5. Repeat these last 3 steps again and again and again, until you begin to feel that they are merging. You will start to feel that whilst focusing on one improvement, your body is automatically looking after the other improvement(s) without your attention.

You must make sure that you keep alternating your focus areas, to keep each improvement fresh in the mind when focusing on a different improvement. Be careful not to think about the previous focus – it should automatically start lingering subconsciously after a while. That is how they will gradually percolate through to the other exercises.

Off Cones Freestyle

Most people who decide to have a go at slalom have never tried freestyle without cones. Their first exposure to the challenge of freestyle is almost totally based around the success criteria of 'did I knock the cone?' If they didn't knock the cone, great, if they did, they need to make sure they don't next time. Having this as their only experience of freestyle is horrible. It's no wonder that some moves seem difficult and awkward, they feel a lack of power in their slalom, crane over clumsily, and lack a feeling of flow. It is incredibly hard to gain these qualities without ever feeling those qualities away from the preoccupation of not knocking cones.

The solution to this is quite simple. You move away from the cones, and just do the same slalom tricks that you were doing anyway, starting with the basics and moving up.

Power

You will notice that you get more of a pumping feeling in your body during the simpler moves like Crisscross – go with that. Try to exaggerate that feeling, start trying to see how big you can make your skating, maybe even make some sounds with your skates. Really feel the force between your skates and the ground. Think of something that frustrates you and try to use the move that you are doing to express it – perhaps this will cause you to fall out of the move, but who cares? Have a go with various moves, whilst striving for a feeling of wanton abandon, pushing the limits of size, force and power further and further.

Head

When you are not needing to avoid annoying cone-shaped objects on the floor, you will find that there really is no other reason to look down, providing you are on a relatively smooth and uninteresting patch of ground. Ice skaters and hockey players rarely look at their feet because their floor is possibly the most predictable of all, and as a result their form is much better. Not looking at your feet also gives you a feeling of the move, instead of a feeling of scrutinising the move. Just let the move happen from your muscle memory and really try to experience how it feels – during the Crazy, feel your body swaying like a pendulum, during the Italian feel your body twisting and untwisting like an elastic band. You will notice things that you'd never thought about whilst on the cones, but the new discoveries and feelings will stay with you when you return.

Weight transfer

When doing slalom, as has been previously beaten to death, it's important to have nice and clean transfers of weight from one foot to the other, at the correct moment. Well, how about we scrap the 'correct moment in relation to the cones' bit, and just go for switching when it feels right instead. The Crazy and Mabrouk are great examples of when this can be useful. Just do the move, and allow your body to rotate as much or as little as it chooses during these (or other) moves, falling from one foot to the other whenever your body feels like toppling over and being saved by the other foot. Once you have relaxed into this toppling as and when it feels good, it is remarkably easy to rein it in to work in the context of the cones again.

Freestyling off cones allows a completely different focus. By moving away from cones, you have taken away probably the most important 80% of what you were thinking about. We all like to think that we were trying to feel more power etc. when we were slaloming, but, actually, we were just seeing what we could get whilst also doing the move correctly around the cones. By robbing ourselves of our central focus, all we have left is the beauty of the move itself, and our preoccupation will automatically shift onto the 'luxury' qualities such as the feelings of power and flow.

3 times per move

When practising, we often find that after some improvement things take a bit of a downhill turn. This leads to frustration and then things only get worse. The more you practise one move, the more you reinforce any bad habits that you may be nurturing, such as bending over during the Screw, or putting weight on a foot that you shouldn't. This isn't really what anyone wants to hear, since, we're supposed to practise one move over and over in order to get better. So what is the solution?

The solution is to only practise as many times as you can fully concentrate. According to Dan Millman, this magical number is 3. Do the move or combo 3 times. And then rest – change something. Maybe you want to alternate with another move, maybe you want to take a lap of the area you are in or maybe you simply want to watch whilst a practice partner does their 3 goes (a very useful exercise) – whatever you do, give your body a little change. I always favoured alternating heel wheeling with toe wheeling when learning them. If I didn't, then I would just 'lose it' after a while.

Organising Practice

Organising your practice sessions

Everyone has their own method of arranging a practice session, and there is no right or wrong way. I mean, this isn't school is it – it's your hobby. Even calling it a 'practice session' is slightly … schoolish, perhaps we should just call it 'slaloming'? But many of us are motivated by learning – each time we do an activity we love practising it and feeling improvement, so it pretty much is a 'practice session', but one that is more related to pleasure than any kind of competitive aim.

However, after the initial learning curve has deserted us, and improvement isn't quite as 'leaps and bounds' as it used to be, motivation may start flagging a little. We might start turning up to skate wondering what we should do in order for us to get our next fix (feeling of improvement/learning/success) and then when a fix is not quick in coming, we may just sit around or chat, not really knowing what to do. Since we have so many things that we need to improve, we just don't know where to start – the task is too huge.

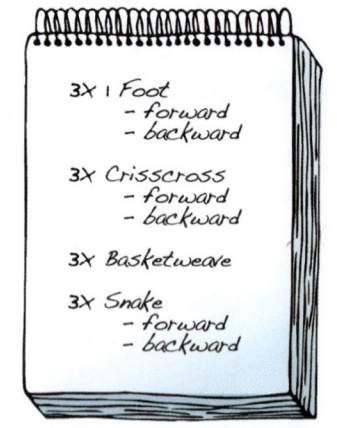

The answer is to focus slightly. Just like we need to focus on a few improvements to a move, and only work on one of them at any one time, we need to rein in our focus when it comes to what we should do in our practice sessions.

As we get better and better there are various things we need to do to keep increasing our level:
- Keep improving and developing our already-known moves
- Find and learn new moves
- Improve our high technical skills and tricks
- Make and practise combos for competition preparation

There may be others that are specific to you, too. Turning up to skate and not knowing which of these to work on is frustrating. Instead, split your session into these four sections and devote each section to one of these areas. Then, within those areas, again split them up. It might look something like:
- Keep improving and developing moves you already know
    - Drift – try to get the entry smoother
    - Italian – speed it up so it can keep to the beat of disco music
    - Wiper – smooth it out, make it less frantic
- Find and learn new moves
    - The trick videos on the PMP (Portable Multimedia Player)
    - Most wanted high technical tricks improvement and development
    - Backward toe wheeling on left toe
    - Swan
    - Counter clockwise heel spin on right heel

- Make and practise combos for competition preparation
  - Make and practise 50cm run
  - Make and practise 120cm run
  - Make and practise two 80cm runs

Suddenly you've got a whole load of goals and mini projects there, all of which you can work on in just a 2-hour session without feeling bored. Little and often is the key. Any one day you might spend the first 30 minutes playing with the improvements in the first section, 3 times the Drift, 3 times the Italian, 3 times the Wiper, and repeat … (you will be amazed at how soon 30 minutes flies by when you have a focus). Then get out your video player or however it is that you intend to try out a new move – I usually have a piece of paper with crazy looking diagrams with arrows, feet and scrawled directions on it. Spend 30 minutes trying to work it out, and playing with it, seeing what it could combine with etc before switching to your technical drills.

I call these drills for a reason – that is just what it is like. It's not like other moves where you can feel wanton abandon as you practise sometimes – highly technical moves need to be done in a very considered manner to prevent bad habits with posture from creeping in. I recommend keeping the same drills for ages – at least a month because it takes time to really improve them to a respectable degree. During these 30 minutes you need to keep yourself calm and away from frustration. For the examples I gave I would suggest the following drills:

- Forward toe wheeling through 10 x 50cm cones (3 times, breather, then repeat)
- Back Crisscross, and finish the last 3 cones on left toe wheel only. (3 times, breather, then repeat)
- Repeat these two drills until 10 minutes is up
- Toe-toe Snake through 10 x 80cm cones, focusing on slow, exaggerated shapes (3 times)
- Toe-toe Snake for a few cones, and then allow the body to fold down into the swan, looking around to the next cone, and allowing the body to follow the gaze like an unwinding elastic band, before reverting to toe-toe Snake (3 times)
- As above but allowing the swan to continue for two cones before continuing in Snake (3 times or unless failed before 3 are completed, in which case swan drills start again from beginning)
- If the previous drill is successful, go for 3 cones, and so on.
- Spend 10 minutes on the above drills
- Heel wheeling through 50cm cones (3 times, breather, repeat)
- Try the heel spin once for each focus (killing speed, position of air leg, arms, torso, head, etc) and then repeat from start.

Now you have an agenda, with a plan for when tricks don't work, other than 'try again, whilst wanting to kick cones'. It also means that you are building up your higher technical level tricks using healthy foundations each time. When concentrating you only need to spend 10 minutes on a technical improvement to get what you can out of it that session. Stopping before spending much longer on it also prevents bad habits becoming too ingrained.

In the final 30 minutes you might want to focus on your next competition - so, how about working entirely on the 50cm line? Run through all the tricks that you could do in the 50cm line while listening to your proposed soundtrack, and get working on putting a combo together. Tomorrow you can either finish the choreography or move onto the 120cm line.

By splitting your practice sessions into different sections with different focuses, you are breaking down the huge mountain of improvement into more manageable hills. If you want to break them down even further, as I have described, then you are giving yourself a bit of a flight of stairs with which to climb those hills. It is much better for giving yourself a sense of direction and goals than just turning up and slaloming without much focus.

Monthly Projects and Themes

Practice and development need to be freshened up now and then to keep you motivated. It is a good idea to change your area of focus or theme each month. Create monthly projects for yourself and then even if you fall off the 'practice wagon' you will be able to get back on again at the next month change. Having a monthly focus also means that you will see much faster improvement in that area than you would if you did not intensively focus on it for a period of time.

The winter is a great time to work on your fundamentals and style, so why not set January aside to work on those jerky arms of yours? You will still continue to do all of your other slalom and work on new tricks etc however you will also have this intensive project running alongside.

Then in February you might want to really brush up your wheelings. You would probably be working on them anyway, but having them as a special project for the month will see a much faster improvement as you pay special attention to those associated exercises and drills for the month.

Other ideas for monthly projects are:
- any style improvement;
- copying someone's competition combo from which you want to learn the style or tricks (NB: copying another skater's combo is just as welcomed as copying tricks, but be sure not to pass it off as your own work and use it for a competition!);
- learning as many tricks as you can on your less-natural side;

- working on your foundations;
- increasing your speed.

This list isn't exhaustive but should give you a few ideas to get your mind working.

Getting Frustrated?

Depending on your personality type, you're likely to get frustrated when practising sometimes. Perhaps you were great at a trick yesterday but can't pull it off today or maybe your patience is starting to wear thin with a trick that just won't work. Whatever the reason, we all get it and you need to snap out of it before:

- your enjoyment of what you are doing starts to wane and you start regarding practice as an unpleasant means to an end;
- your motor patterns start to develop bad habits; and
- your frustration makes you less able to pull anything off – thus making you angry and even less able to skate well.

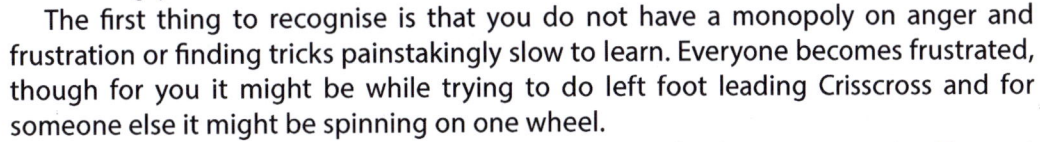

The first thing to recognise is that you do not have a monopoly on anger and frustration or finding tricks painstakingly slow to learn. Everyone becomes frustrated, though for you it might be while trying to do left foot leading Crisscross and for someone else it might be spinning on one wheel.

Next you need to reset yourself so that you can get back to your practice. To reset yourself there are several things you can do:

- Do whatever you are attempting in ultra slow motion (see Slow Motion practice technique on p 110). This will bring your centre of gravity back down and get your knees being used more again, among other things.
- Run through your basics working on style. The chances are that the quality of your slalom has taken a hit, thus affecting your ability to do your top tricks. Working on your style with the basics should sort this out.
- Run through some drills off cones.
- Work on the skills or tricks which support the trick you are working on, such as toe-toe tricks if you are working on Swan.
- Simply start working on something else, however the chances are that you need to reset yourself first. Calm down using something happy and familiar or repetitive.

It may also be that your brain is fatigued for that day and those motor neurons need to be rested in order to repair and strengthen, just like your muscles need recovery time to do the very same thing.

PREPARING FOR COMPETITIONS

Types of competition 123

Classic Competitions 125
    Judging

Battle Competitions 127
    Judging

Preparing for a Classic Competition 130
    Before the comp
    Finalising the combo
    Perfecting the combo

Preparing for a Battle 137
    Before the comp
    Improvising for Battle
    Last Trick

Tactics 139

The Day of The Competition 140

The Results 142

PREPARING FOR COMPETITIONS

You have probably avoided this part of the book because you don't think it's for you – you're just slaloming for fun, for no one but yourself and you're not interested in competing. You're not all full of yourself and you have nothing to prove ….

If this is how you are currently thinking then you should take the time to think again. It isn't about showing off or putting yourself up on a pedestal on which to embarrass yourself; it is, instead, about taking part and more like a glorified karaoke night or a show-and-tell party between friends.

Once you have taken part you will see that at competitions there is a difference between those who take part and those who don't. Those who take part are part of the party, part of an exclusive club of skaters and friends, whatever their level, and I have very rarely come across anyone who has been unsure about taking part and not felt absolutely delighted about having gone and given it a go. Particularly when everything went wrong for them – it makes you feel alive and part of the occasion.

You could say that 'competitions' are pretty much just a fun skate event where slalom skaters can get together and play together with a tournament as the central format.

Types of competition

There are two main styles of competition being used in the world at the moment for freestyle slalom: Classic style and Battle style competitions.

'Classic' style is the original style which started back in the 1990s in Europe. Similar to many Olympic sports, each skater has an opportunity to give a usually pre-prepared presentation to a panel of judges. Points are given which are used to give the skaters their competition ranking.

'Battle' style is a more recent development, that started in 2005. Based on the competition style of other street sports, such as BMX flatland, competitors are put into groups and fight it out within those groups, with about half of each group proceeding through to the next round. This continues until the final group when the remaining riders are ranked.

Classic Competitions

The competition area consists of 54 cones, made up of 3 lines with each line having cones set out at a different spacing – 50cm, 80cm and 120cm. The lines for 50cm and 80cm consist of 20 cones, and the cone line for 120cm is only 14 cones.

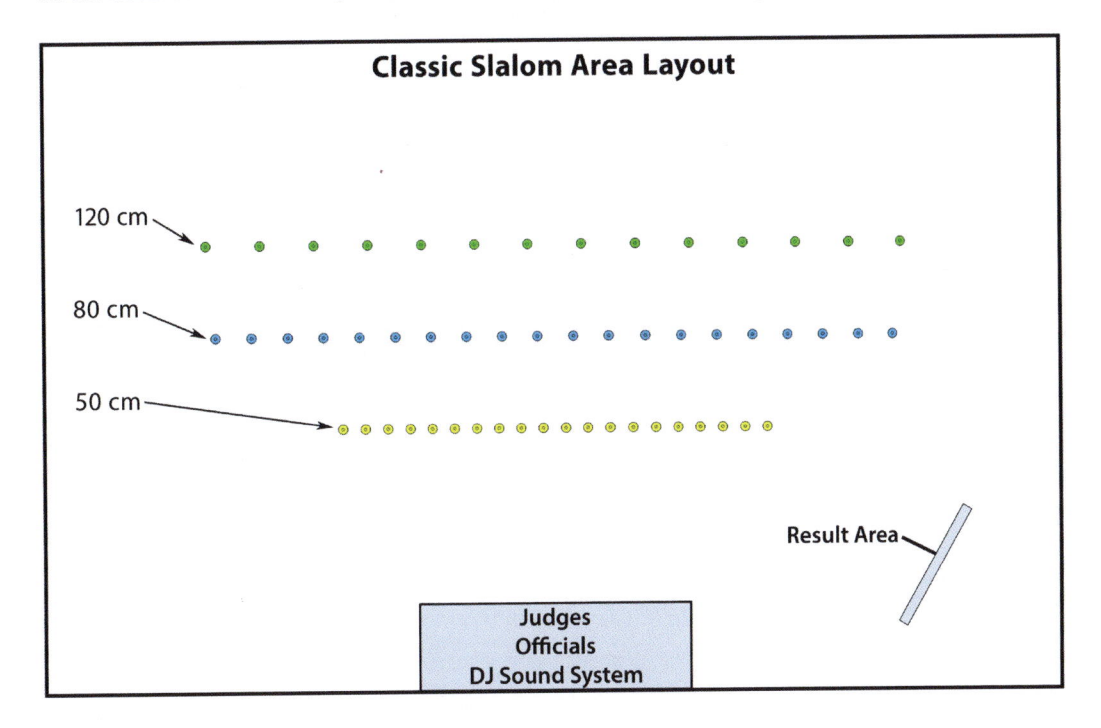

Classic Slalom Area Layout

- 120 cm
- 80 cm
- 50 cm
- Result Area
- Judges / Officials / DJ Sound System

Each rider selects their own music to play, and has 105 to 120 seconds from the start of the music during which to pass through all of the cones, showing their slalom.

Judging

In Classic style, there is a panel of at least 3 judges, each of whom has the responsibility of awarding a score for each rider, independent of the other judges. Each of the scores is then collated and processed, and an eventual final score for each rider emerges.

The judging categories are split into 'Technique' and 'Artistic', with 50 points available for each category, with a maximum score of 100 overall.

The Technical category is further divided into 3 sections:
- Trick Difficulty
- Continuity
- Speed

Variety

This evaluates the diversity in the rider's slalom. The judges will note down whether or not the rider is able to integrate spinning tricks, wheeling, sitting tricks and jumping tricks into their slalom performance.

Continuity

This evaluates how well the rider combines tricks together. Is the rider's base level of a good quality which allows them to move continuously whilst switching from one trick to the next? Are the high difficulty tricks blended well into the rest of the slalom?

Speed

This evaluates how the speed of the riders slalom is affecting the technical difficulty of what they are doing. Similarly, if changes in speed are done smoothly, free of starts and stops, it indicates a sound control of the tricks performed. Tricks done in time with the rhythm of the music also demonstrates technical achievement.

The Artistic category is also further divided into 3 sections:
- Body performance
- Music expression
- Trick management

Body performance

This evaluates the rider's ability to blend body movement into the skating, rather than leaving the body stiff whilst the feet and legs do all the work. This criterion recognises that whilst a beginner will often concentrate mainly on the feet, a more advanced skater should be paying increased attention to the arms, head and body when slaloming.

Music expression

This evaluates how much the rider is matching their skating and tricks to the mood of the music – the blending of the body movement with the music is taken into account here.

Trick management

This evaluates the extent to which the choreography matches the breaks and changes in the music. It also recognises that 'technical highlights' are more difficult at different stages in a performance, such as in the middle of a line of cones instead of at the start or finish of a cone line.

Penalties

- Falling: 2.5–3.5 points
- Timing: 10 points for finishing before 105 seconds or after 120 seconds
- Cone knocking: 0.5 points for each cone hit or not slalomed.

Battle Competitions

The arrangement is 4 lines: 20 cones at 50cm spacing; 20 cones at 80cm spacing; 14 cones at 120cm spacing; and 10 cones at 80cm spacing. In Battle competitions there is no obligation to pass through all of the cones. In fact, a rider could slalom around one cone for their entire competition and not face any penalty, though it would be difficult to show much slalom ability if doing so.

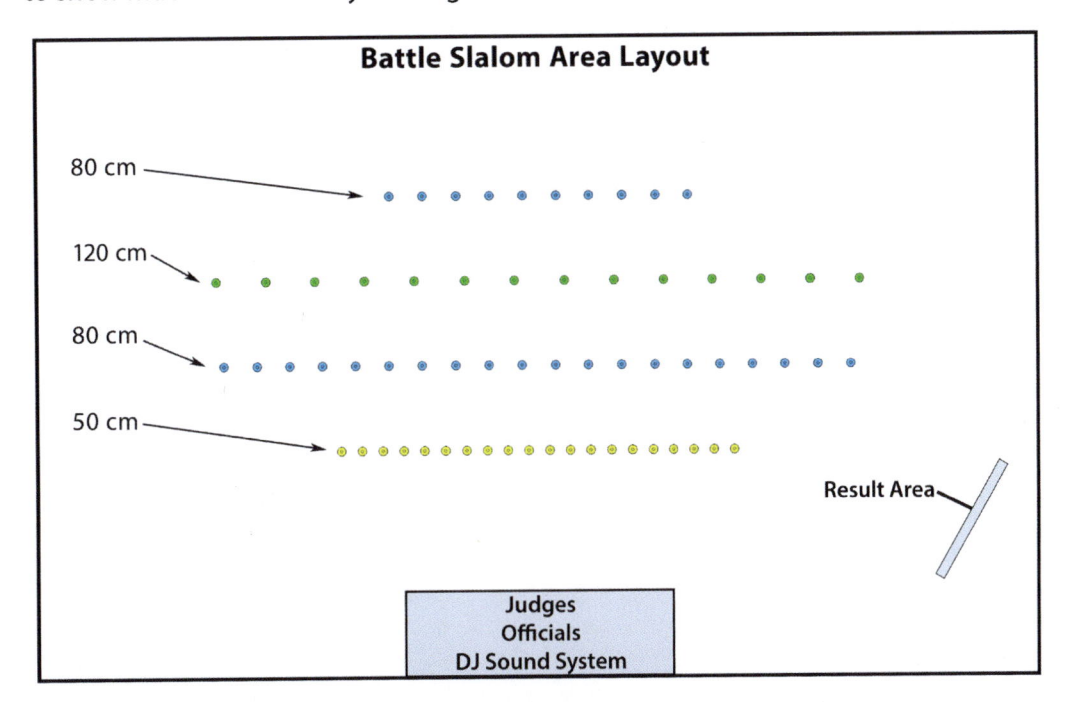

Battle Slalom Area Layout

The Battle competition is a knock-out style tournament, where participants are initially split into battle groups of 3-5 riders. First-round battle groups are decided based on the seeding of the riders and aim to create equal battle groups, keeping the highest seeded riders from knocking each other out until the later rounds.

During each battle the riders will take it in turns to skate for 30-second runs in the cones and each rider will get two or three runs before the end of the battle. In the final round, there is usually an additional 'last trick' run where each rider has the opportunity to show one final trick, along with the option of a second attempt if the first took less than 10 seconds.

At the end of each battle the top two riders are announced to go through to the next round, and the other riders drop from the competition. This continues until the Final, where the top 4 riders are ranked 1st through to 4th.

During the battles a DJ will play music continually and the riders do not have any choice in what gets played during their battle.

Judging

In Battle style there is a panel of three judges, each of whom rank the skaters at the end of each round. Once the judges have completed their individual rankings, comparisons between them are made, disparities are discussed and a final rank is confirmed and announced.

The disparities between the judges' rankings are usually settled quickly with each judge stating their case and compromising or re-thinking. Sometimes, however, the panel is unable to come to a settlement, and two or more riders may be asked to show one 'best trick' as a tie breaker. Fortunately this is rare since it always makes the competition organiser worry about the competition finishing on time!

No scores are given during Battle competitions since the judges' opinion of the correct ranking is the most important factor, however many variables are considered during the making of the judges' rankings.

Penalties

Since Battle competitions do not use a points scoring system, kicked cones and falls are simply 'taken into account' by the judges. If a skater performs a trick where some of the cones are knocked over, the trick is considered as a slalom trick only for the cones which remained upright. If a skater executes a challenging manoeuvre or trick but knocks over the cone(s), it is recognised that they are able to perform the trick outside of the cone line.

Falls are not the 'be all or end all' that some may think, and there are no penalties for cones not slalomed, since in Battle competitions the riders only skate the cones that they choose.

The Ranking

Battles are judged very differently to the more artistic based Classic competitions. They are judged on how technically difficult the displayed slalom is, however this is not the same as judging based on the technical difficulty of the tricks attempted or executed by the skater.

Battle judging is very much about doing the tricks, but is also about finishing them off and being able to link them with other skating besides Crisscross or other run-up/recovery tricks and maintaining the general flow of the slalom. No marks are awarded or scores given since the judges simply rank the skaters within the battle group, however the following unofficial factors are taken into account when ranking:

Finishing off tricks

If a skater shows a trick of which they maintain control from the start of the trick until the end of the trick, it shows a greater technical achievement than if a skater loses control of the trick during execution, and 'collapses' out of it, even if each trick lasted a similar length of time or number of cones.

Continuity and flow

If a skater executes a sitting trick, then abruptly stands up before doing some freestyle, followed by pushing off to gain momentum for a wheeling exit from the cones, this shows a lower technical achievement than another skater who is able to transition smoothly between the different phases of their run.

Integration with other freestyle

Tricks which are not integrated well into other freestyle slalom show a lower technical achievement overall and also for those tricks. If a technically difficult trick is entered from more freestyle instead of from a clear set-up, this shows a greater risk taken by the skater. The same works for the trick-exit – it shows a good mastery of the trick if the skater is able to transition well from the trick itself into something other than a basic trick.

Range of tricks

If a skater covers a wide range of tricks instead of just focusing on one skill such as being able to play around on one or two wheels, then it shows technical achievement in a range of different types of skills.

An example of this would be someone who shows a strong focus on only wheeling tricks. They might show a lower technical level than another skater who does some wheeling but also shows that they have taken the time to train many other non-wheeling or more creative tricks.

Preparing for a Classic Competition

Before the comp

There is no obligation to have a prepared combo for a Classic style competition. Many of us have chosen music on the day and improvised our way through a 105 second Classic run. Sometimes the judges can tell and sometimes they can't, but that is not your concern since they will judge on what they see and not on whether they think you have been planning it. However there are advantages to planning a combo, and I highly recommend it:

- If your skating is clearly choreographed to the music, demonstrated by the occasional trick or stall which fits the highlights of the music, then this is judged favourably under the 'trick management' and 'musical expression' areas.
- If you have created a combo then you are likely to have included all of your most impressive tricks, appropriately spread between the 3 lines of cones and you are far less likely to forget to include certain tricks – as is very common when improvising under the haze of nerves.
- If you practise the same combo over and over before a competition, then you are less likely to knock over cones or repeat the same low level tricks over and over between your 'show tricks'.

In short, if you would like to show yourself at your best in a Classic style competition, you will need a combo. This is a greatly procrastinated task by many skaters and is easy for none of us, so it is best to get started as soon as possible, giving you more time for fine tuning and practice. You should aim to have your combo prepared two months before a competition in order to have time to practise it and become completely relaxed with your body whilst doing it. This may seem excessive, but once you have your individual runs planned, then skating them all together is an entirely different experience – it can be very exhausting, leaving you sloppy and shaky for your final 30 seconds. It is also important to practise it enough beforehand because when you start skating prepared combos instead of improvising, you will find that a fair amount of your power and energy has transformed into mechanical awkwardness. This is very frustrating. Rest assured that after enough practice this will reverse, and you will eventually have more power and energy than before. Kicking of cones is also something which might have almost stopped at some point during your practice, but will still happen during your competition. Practise even more to make the kicking of cones almost an impossibility – then you shall get away with only a few in the competition itself.

Here are some tips to get you going with making your combo:

Timing

You have 105 to 120 seconds to play with, so aim for 110 seconds. You have 3 lines of cones and you will probably visit one or more of the lines at least twice, so you need to allow time for catching your breath and skating from one line of cones to the next. Start out by working with about 7 seconds between lines, so that's about 20 of your 110 seconds gone already, plus whatever intro time you have after your music has started. If you allow 10 seconds for the 120cm line, 20 seconds for the 50s, and spend the rest of the time on a couple of runs through the 80s, then you shouldn't find yourself going way over time in your first test run of your completed combo.

Music

There are more songs available to you than there are tricks, making this one of the most difficult choices when preparing a combo. It is strongly advised that you pick your music before making your combo, since then your combo can match the natural breaks and highlights in the music. If you are really stuck however, you can just go ahead and make a combo and just see what songs and beats work well with your skating nearer to the time of the competition.

Start by making a shortlist of tracks. It should be something you like! It should also have a similar style to the skating that you wish to show, i.e. if your style is very strong and angry then pick a strong and angry track, and if your style is very smooth and graceful without much beat, then something more easy listening might be more appropriate. Most people find that something with more of a beat works best for them, so unless you have any strong feelings, I recommend going for something with a beat, highlights and changes to add interest to your run and allow for different moods for different lines. If you make a note of some tracks which work, you can count the beats per minute and then search for other tracks with similar timing. Put up to ten favourites in a play list for your headphones whilst slaloming.

When skating with your shortlist, you will gradually start to eliminate tracks when you find them too constant in tone, too fast or slow, or not upbeat enough. Perhaps you just find that you no longer like certain tracks after skating to them so much – get rid of these! You are selecting a track to be your constant companion for the coming months ….

Once your track is chosen, go through it several times, noting down the times when the music changes, has highlights, has instrumental sections, vocals etc. You may find that there is a convenient 90-second section with conveniently placed 5-10 second rest sections, separated by exciting upbeat sections for your runs. However, this is unlikely, so either you will need to be more flexible with matching your combo perfectly to the music, or you can play around with editing the track. Editing a track to fit your skating can be fun, but first you must make your combo. Either way, it is now time to put your chosen track on endless repeat and create your runs.

What your combo should be

Your combo should obviously be full of your tricks, and of course you should consider the technical level of those tricks. Trick level is not the only thing judged however! Take a look back at the Judging section for Classic style (p 125) and you will see that there are 6 criteria which are examined by the judges other than timing and penalties. They all have rather open descriptions which often overlap with each other, so here is a quick and simplified checklist to keep at the front of your mind whilst planning your combo:

- Variety – make sure you cover a number of trick families.
- Continuity – use transitions which enable you to flow continuously from trick to trick instead of causing unintentional stalling.
- Speed – include tricks and transitions which you can do at a reasonable pace. Watch out for inelegant slowing when doing something more technically difficult.
- Body Performance – If you can't do a trick or transition without looking very awkward, it might be best to leave it out.
- Music Expression – Keep the mood of the music in mind.
- Trick Management – Plan your tricks to fit the timing of the changes in the music.

Getting started

Your mind is probably swimming at this point, with no idea where to start. Perhaps your mind keeps going blank when you try to think of all the tricks you know and want to include. Here is one technique to get things moving:

- Take a sheet of paper and start writing down all the tricks, transitions or skills that you would quite like to include or show that you can do. They don't need names, you can even write 'the sliding thing where I point at my friends while doing it'. I say 'start' writing down the tricks because you'll usually find yourself adding to them over a few days as you remember more and more tricks that didn't come to mind at the time.
- Once you have a list, mark the ones that you can do on 50cm cones, which ones you can do on 120cm cones, and which ones must be done on 80cm cones. Now you are starting to split them up into potential runs.
- Get another sheet of paper and rewrite the list into 3 columns
    - tricks that you definitely must include
    - tricks that you would very much like to include
    - tricks that can be used if appropriate
- Now you are ready to start combining the tricks. Take a look over the lists and start spotting tricks that you usually put together – by this time you will have skated a lot to this music. Draw a line connecting the two. Continue like this until you have all of your usual mini-combos noted.
- On a fresh sheet, note down these mini-combos, then cross off these tricks from the 3-column list to see what you have remaining. You are already starting to choreograph before you have even put on your skates or played your music.
- Get your skates on, put your music on repeat, and take to the cones with the 3-column list in your hand. You might want to start out with the 50cm line, as it is usually the most difficult to prepare since you will skate this distance a lot less than the more typical 80cm line. Or you might prefer to start on the 80cm line because it's an easier start. Just play around with the cones and the music,

taking each of the tricks or transitions in the first column and skating them. Take a note of which tricks you enjoyed transitioning from before the trick in question and which ones you enjoyed transitioning into afterwards. You want to keep to your natural movements as much as possible, so seeing what you naturally choreograph is a good start! If it helps, try setting up a video camera and just skating to your music in the line of cones, checking your list and including as many of the tricks as you can. Then you can play it back and see which bits you like and which you don't.
- By this time you're well on your way to getting some runs together. Make sure that you are not just connecting difficult tricks – the flow of the runs are as important as the tricks that you are doing, so pay close attention to the transitions.

120cm cone line

The 120cm line is usually the quickest as it is the spacing which was used at places such as the Trocadero in Paris, where skaters zipped through at high speeds, switching between the faster tricks such as Crisscross, Snake, 1-Foot and Side-surf ('old school' style of slalom). At my first competition I did far slower and intricate movements and was told that the judges wanted to see more old school style in the 120s. This isn't the case anymore and there are no expectations of what you should do, however it is a nice opportunity to up the speed and whoosh through with whichever tricks you can switch between at speed. The 120cm line is also useful for tricks which you have not yet mastered well enough to include in the 80cm spacing or just don't flow quite as well in such a tight spacing – such as sitting moves and 'Running Independents'.

50cm cone line

The 50cm line originally came from Italy and, like the 120cm line, was only adopted by other countries when efforts were made to unite and standardise slalom in all countries. 50cm spaced cones lend themselves to the more sideways tricks although most other tricks can be done in this spacing too. Traditionally, Wiper, Jumping X, Nelson style of tricks would be done in this line, along with some Crazy Legs and other dance style movements. Nowadays the 50cm line is also very suitable for heel or toe wheeling because constant and regular direction changes are required, helping to sustain the balance. Whatever you do on the 50cm cones, don't go crazy with taking risks, since this is the line which tends to lose the most cones during a competition due to the reduced room for error.

80cm cone line

The 80cm line is the easiest to find tricks for since you have probably learned most of your slalom on this spacing, and practise almost completely on it too. If you skate in a location where you have to mark your cone line down every time you skate, then you are likely to rarely take the time to mark a 50cm or 120cm line too. You will also probably pick the 80cm line as the one to re-visit if you have time for a 4th run through a line of cones during your combo. Powerful tricks tend to be most at home in the

80cm line because it gives you more room for error than the 50cm line, and more time for big carves and sideways movement than the 120cm line.

Finalising the combo

Once you have runs planned for your combo, you need to finalise everything and make any adjustments needed to get it all flowing smoothly. You will need to go through each run to the music many, many times so that you can see which tricks or transitions are not settling in as you had expected. Sometimes it is a transition, sometimes it is a whole trick. Sometimes you need to retire a trick from an entire combo because the beat of the music is too fast for you to do it comfortably. If a transition is not working you may, perhaps, just need to elongate it a bit so that it takes up more cones. When this happens, or you need to replace a transition, it can change all of your spacing and your run no longer fits the cone line – it happens to everyone and is very frustrating, so the process can continue for a while.

You may find that a highly technical trick you have put into the run may not be ready in time for the competition, or maybe its success depends on the type and quality of the skating surface. If this is the case then you could have a reserve trick to take its place in case the first choice trick needs to be pulled at the last minute.

The next step is to set up all 60 cones and skate it together, in time with the music, under competition time constraints. When you are doing this, you must not stop if it all goes wrong! You must continue until the end of your combo, keeping to the time constraints as you would do if it all went wrong in a competition. The chances are that you will have run out of breath after your very first line of cones and then proceeded to hit many more cones than normal. If this happens, take time to survey the wreckage and pat yourself on the back for preparing your combo so conscientiously in advance that you have time to improve it …

Small changes might need to be made at this point – perhaps some of the breaks between lines need to be a bit longer, or perhaps the lines need to be executed in a different order because you are too exhausted for some tricks after 70 seconds.

Perfecting the combo

Once you have a completed combo, it is time to make sure that you are able to do it on the day. There are two phases to this:
- Phase 1 is where you practise to become good enough at your combo that you can competently execute it in time with the music, without hitting the cones.
- Phase 2 is where you become so experienced and good at your combo that not only do you look and feel natural and powerful whilst doing it, but you gradually reduce the chances of hitting each cone under competition pressure.

During Phase 1, you will find your progress having ups and downs, with the first down being when you realise that you have made the wrong combo – it doesn't suit you or display your skating to its best at all. Don't panic, this is normal. When you allow your movements to flow naturally it will feel powerful and the natural flow will be evident. When you chart those movements on paper and then deliberately execute them to music, it will often feel contrived and awkward for the first fifty or so times.

You will also find during Phase 1 that you start becoming less exhausted as your specific fitness is developed. If you want to improve even more, try giving yourself only 30 seconds rest between two run-throughs of your combo.

During Phase 2 you should start working on the style more, and also make things as difficult as possible for yourself.

Many of the tips given in the 'Practice' section are also applicable to a competition combo:

- Try doing it 3 times before taking a longer rest or talking to anyone. Allow yourself long enough to physically recover between each run-through, but not long enough to lose focus.
- At the start of any practice session or if you feel your learning curve going down instead of up, run through your combo in ultra slow motion instead.
- Whether your skating surface is level or not, alternate the end that you start from. This will change things psychologically for you. This is very useful for shaking things up for yourself during Phase 2.

Once you are into Phase 2, there are some extra techniques which you might want to use. If you are finding Phase 1 a little tedious and non-motivating, go ahead and use these techniques for that too.

- Slow your combo down and skate it to a slower but strong beat. Disco music often works well for this. It can be frustrating to slow your skating down but persevere until you can feel your body enjoying the slower beat and making more expressive movements as a result.
- Speed your combo up and skate it to a faster beat. You will probably lose all quality but it will make you grateful for your regular music afterwards. Think of it as resistance training.
- Play around with the skating surface and levels. If your surface is completely level, try practising somewhere that it is not, and alternate the directions that you skate from, as per the earlier tip. Try to also find a location where the surface is different to your usual surface – if you find this more difficult, great! Better now than on the day.
- If you are upset about something, it can have a severe effect on your slalom. Practise blocking external emotions out whilst you skate your combo, and become more experienced at focusing more exclusively on the cones and the current movement.
- Try to get your friends to stand and watch you wherever possible. The pressure makes things so much harder.
- Set up a camera so that you can see areas where your arms fly, you look awkward, or something else just doesn't look right or needs improving.

Little and often is the key for perfecting a combo, so try to run through your combo every day if possible. Just one time is enough to get your body and mind processing it in the background for you while you are getting on with the rest of your life. If you can run through it 6 times, great, but if you only have time for once then it is much better than waiting until you have time to do more.

Lastly, a quick reminder that during practice you must always complete the full combo and salvage it as best as you can, however wrong it goes – just as you would do in a competition.

Preparing for a Battle

Before the comp

Battle competitions are traditionally improvised, and done without having pre-planned combos. In fact, some skaters consider making a combo for a Battle competition to be cheating – I don't agree with this. I think that having pre-prepared combos can make a competition duller and not so exciting, but I also believe that it can make the experience much less intimidating for first timers, and can help the reliability of performing tricks.

When you get to the higher levels of competition though, your performance will be lacking if you have prepared it all beforehand. You only need to watch the men's battle finals in a major competition to appreciate the authenticity and added charisma of an improvised run.

Making combos for Battle

If you do decide to make a combo, take a look through the section about preparing for Classic Style competitions (p 130) – it will explain a way of making runs which can also be used for Battle. You can ignore the information about music and covering all 3 lines of cones but you should still consider speed, continuity, body movement and variety. Another difference between Classic and Battle combos is that with Battle you will want to put in as many tricks as you can – so worry less about creating a beautiful composition and more about stuffing it full of your best tricks. Take a look back at the judging criteria for Battle competitions (p 128).

For timing, just make sure that none of your runs last more than 30 seconds and have a few 5-10 second filler tricks or mini combos for when you finish a little early and can fill in some time. For example if you can do wheelings then it is a good time for them, or maybe you could zip down the 120cm line with sitting tricks. A trick that you cannot yet link to others could also be used in those final few seconds of a run.

You won't usually know how many runs you will have in each round until the day of the competition so you will need to plan for different situations. Usually it will be two or three, with two in the first round and three in the later rounds. Some first round groups can be very difficult so put everything into just two 30-second runs. You might want to consider choreographing two runs and enjoy improvising a third if you get the chance.

Improvising for Battle

If you are going to improvise your battle runs then you can just ignore the rest of this bit, just turn up to the competition and see what happens. However, there are techniques that you can use to help make the experience less stressful and more fruitful.

When practising before the competition write down a list of tricks that you would like to include as if you were preparing by making combos. Each time you go into the cones pick approximately 3 tricks that you want to have done by the time you leave the cones. If it is the first time you have done something like this you may find it challenging. A great warm-up exercise is to zip through the cones, switching from forward to backward to forward again with absolutely no plan – it is very good for practising your improvisation skills. With practice you will find it easier and easier to find your way from one trick to another whilst maintaining continuity as you do so.

Remember when you are improvising that it is not just your tricks that you are showing off – you are also demonstrating your ability to flow comfortably inside the cones.

When you go for your competition you will find it handy to have a list of tricks tucked into your pocket so you can remind yourself of what you can do, just in case your mind goes blank with nerves. If you learned something new that day, feel free to pop that into the mix too. Other tricks which you should include in your mix are ones which you see your fellow battlers doing – it is very much in the spirit of battle to match or raise someone else's trick.

Last Trick

During the early years of Battle competitions every round would have three runs and a last trick, but nowadays the last trick is usually only used during the final. This part of the competition gives you the opportunity to have up to two attempts at a trick that you feel shows your technical expertise at its best. Here are some things to think about when selecting which trick to show:

- How long it takes – a longer lasting trick is much more of a crowd pleaser, but you must also consider that if it lasts more than 10 seconds then you cannot have a second attempt, and the judges are far more immune to the crowd pleasing effects of a long lasting trick.
- Whether it is new – If you have already used this trick in this round, then it could waste your last trick since you are not showing the judges anything new. If however it is very much better than other tricks that you could show and it deserves a clearer highlight, then you should go ahead with it again anyway.
- If you failed it earlier – if you tried this trick earlier in the round but it went wrong, then now is a good time to show that you can do it much better.
- A risky trick – if you have a trick which you didn't want to include in your main battle rounds because you're at an early stage of learning it and it often goes wrong, or you need to calm yourself before attempting it, then now is a good time to have a go with the knowledge that you can have a second attempt if you need it. Often the more risky tricks such as one-wheel tricks are popular for this reason.
- Battle it out – finally, back to good old battle technique – if you see someone else do a final trick that you can do better, then it can be an easy choice of trick to do. This is especially effective if the competitor in question has a higher world ranking than you.

Tactics

Some tactics have already been mentioned such as matching and raising the tricks of others and making your choice of final trick. Since in the world of freestyle slalom we are not yet at the stage of spiking our opponents' drinks, slipping glue into their bearings or even just throwing the occasional intimidating glare (except in jest, which happens a lot) there is only one major thing left which is considering the most advantageous time to show each trick.

For example, at the start of a competition we are usually very nervous – perhaps not the best time to include our most difficult and risky tricks. You may also find that by the final run your muscles are so exhausted from nerves and skating that you can no longer balance as well on one or two wheels.

You may decide that you would rather use the best part of your first run for relaxing yourself and getting the audience behind you by doing your more dance style movements that are powerful and charismatic. Conversely, you may decide that you would rather get your highly technical tricks out of the way whilst you are fresh, giving you the chance of second attempts in your next run, as and when needed.

Take some time to consider what works best for you. Whether you are preparing combos or improvising your battle runs, try to arrange your tricks in a way which will give you the best results.

One trick placement tactic which can be employed is saving your best tricks for the later rounds. You should be very wary of doing this since the world of freestyle slalom battles can throw some surprising results with highly ranked skaters dropping from the competition when they least expect it. Performing your more difficult tricks earlier in the competition also helps to warm them up before they become vital to your survival. If you do manage to pull it off though, it drives everyone into a frenzy – some of my most memorable moments as a judge have been when someone produces a hidden trick in the final I get so excited I usually start hammering the table and joining in with the exclamations of the spectators

The Day of The Competition

On the day of the competition the most important thing is being able to skate as well as you know that you are able to skate. On a normal day this wouldn't be such a problem for you, but on a competition day the effects of nerves are very wide reaching.

You should expect the usual physical side effects of nerves such as muscular weakness, wobbly legs and tunnel vision when you skate, but also psychological side effects such as feeling out of place, out of depth and being convinced that everyone present is wondering why on earth such an inept slalomer is entering this competition.

Almost all of us have enjoyed every one of these at our first competitions – I was so nervous and ashamed at my first competition that I couldn't orientate myself correctly, only saw the cones as moving and shaking blurs, imagined that everyone was wondering why I was wasting their time and had legs shaking out of control. If it hadn't caused me to fall on the 4th cone like it did, then those effects would have continued for the entire 90 second run. Fortunately I fell thus enabling me to find out just how wrong I was about everyone's sentiment – the crowd went crazy with cheering and applause as I got to my feet and carried on, and for the remainder of the competition there were yells of encouragement and clapping in time with the music. It turned out that everyone was so pleased to see someone experiencing their first competition, as they had once done, that they were all willing the best for me.

Here are some tips on how to deal with competition day nerves:

Arrive at the competition area as early as you can, and get your skates on.

The more time you spend in your skates beforehand, the more at home you will feel in them for the competition. I know this sounds silly because you skate lots and feel at home in them all the time anyway, but this is competition day and you will be surprised how readily nerves will make just skating over to the registration desk seem like something you have yet to master.

Once the area is set up and open for practice, get out there and practise!

This seems like an obvious statement to make, and yes it is. However you will find it very hard to bring yourself to do it before a competition. Most first timers, or anyone with any fear of not being good enough to be there (I still felt this in Asia right up until I retired from competition) will keep procrastinating that first run through the cones. There will be a crowd of seemingly much better, more comfortable and more serious skaters waiting their turn to use the cones, and you will not want to get in their way, waste cone time, or show everyone just how out of your depth you are. You will most likely sit or stand there watching with the feeling that if you tried to take a turn on a cone line, you would be doing the equivalent of running across the tracks halfway through an Olympic 100m sprint race. This is not the case.

Everyone can be a little preoccupied with themselves when warming up for a competition and so won't often think to offer the frightened looking skater a go on the cones, however you will find that if they become aware that you're waiting to have a turn then they'll fall over themselves to encourage you to go ahead and take your time using the line. We all remember the days of fear, and we are all still very grateful that the sport is growing and that competitions are still seeing new participants coming along and joining in. We also have a healthy respect for the fact that the skater who comes along and struggles through Crisscross during their first competition, will probably be wiping the floor with us within two years.

Get comfortable slaloming, and run through your basics

Once you have secured your turn on a cone line it will be almost irresistible to show off your best tricks as a way of establishing your right to be taking part in the competition. Please resist! You will probably try wheeling or something and will fail miserably due to your nerves, thus making you feel worse – clumsy and ashamed. Aim instead for some nice, slow Snake or Crisscross for the first few runs. Forward then backward, then switching, keeping it really nice and slow. This will remind yourself that you are competent, are able to make it through the cone lines without shaking, falling or hitting all of the cones, and will also help you get used to doing something really basic in front of everyone without feeling ashamed about it. I always start out like this and only increase my level of difficulty when relaxed and no longer feeling embarrassed about doing such basic tricks at such an event.

Slow motion practice

As you get more comfortable on the cones you can start running through any combos that you will be using, or practise improvising connecting some tricks that you plan to include. When you do this, try to resist throwing yourself into them full pelt. It may work, but will more likely leave you flustered and wondering where all the cones have gone. Instead, stop worrying about taking up too much time on the cones and skate with wide, exaggerated and slow movements as you progress through your tricks and transitions. Concentrate on your centre of mass, your knee-bend, and your posture. This will calm you down and bring back your confidence and success. When we are nervous we tend to stand up and straighten our legs, making us less stable and bringing our skates closer to the cones – slow down and focus on these elements until you are feeling frustrated with restraint.

Have fun

Once you feel confident again, let yourself go and skate as if you are in your usual skate spot with friends. You will probably be chatting with the others by now so why not take full advantage of the situation and ask to be shown a trick that you've been admiring. This is what these meets are all about – it isn't trophies, it's all about the trick swapping! Skaters who join in the competition usually come away with many more tricks to practise afterwards which they have been enthusiastically shown by other skaters. Everyone loves to be asked to pass on one of their tricks and nothing flatters like seeing it used in competition. This will also take your focus away from the competition, and bring it back to why you are actually at the event.

The Results

This is an important section, because the experience of taking part in a competition can often lead you to deviate from your original intention and accidentally start caring about the result. Perhaps you did very badly and want to find that you just did not come last, or maybe everything went very well and you are keen to see how well you did in relation to the others at the competition. This is all fine and we should take pleasure from doing well in contests such as this, however it can adversely affect your relationship with your pastime.

If you do much worse than expected, it can lead to feelings of frustration and resentment. Frustration that you are not picking up tricks as quickly as others might be, and resentment at others for seeming more naturally gifted than you or having more free time to practise, or having better surfaces and indoor facilities. When you start feeling like this, you need to take stock of yourself before you lose your interest.

If you do much better than expected, as I did in my first competition, it can transform your pleasure-bringing pastime into something which is more about showing off, being quantified, and generally for other people instead of yourself. I won my first competition, in Paris, and spent the next three months training rigorously for the following competition which was in Bordeaux. I was so elated and surprised by my Paris result that I started to wonder just how well I could do, and everything became about the judges and marking scheme. However, I didn't do as well as I had hoped in Bordeaux (I came 4th – just missing out on the podium) and returned to London to watch my interest in skating wane for the rest of the summer. If you skate only for the approval of others then when you fail to impress them, what do you have left?

Finally, it is worth remembering at this point that freestyle slalom is not a quantifiable activity. Like music awards, there will always be plenty of controversy and possible inaccuracy surrounding any results. There is often a trade-off between objectivity and subjectivity when judging slalom. If it is judged purely subjectively then you destroy competition and if it is judged purely objectively then you destroy freestyle slalom: If everything was judged by what tricks and personal style that the particular judges like, then it would make a mockery of competition. Conversely, imagine if there was an ideal combo – everyone would work to try to execute that combo and creativity would die. So freestyle slalom competitions are judged to the best of the judges' ability, whilst following the guidelines of the judging methods shown in this book – however, a different set of judges could come up with different results. It is the nature of such a diverse and creative activity so don't take your perceived success or defeat too much to heart.

About the Author

Naomi Grigg is probably the slalom world's most well-known freestyle instructor.

Having begun skating at age 15, Naomi has experimented in aggressive skating, rhythm skating, speed skating, street skating, roller derby, and has become an internationally famous freestyle slalom skater, peaking at 3rd in the world.

Naomi was the founder and coach of the SkateFreestyle competition and demo team and chairperson of the UK Freestyle Skating Association, working with the British Rolling Sports Federation. Naomi worked extensively to develop the sport both at home in the UK and overseas, and now works to develop slalom skating in her current home, the USA, where she is also the distributor of the SEBA skate brand. She is part of the World Slalom Skaters Association (WSSA) rules technical committee, is a world championships level international judge, and a trainer/certifier of WSSA judges.

Naomi's freestyle slalom résumé includes podium placements in numerous international competitions in Korea, the USA, France, Germany, China, and the Netherlands. When she retired from international competition in 2008, she was the reigning UK champion and was ranked 4th in the world, down from a peak ranking of 3rd.

Beyond the realm of freestyle slalom, Naomi has medalled in speed skating competitions and was the British Marathon Champion in 2005. She played ice hockey with the Swindon Top Cats, competed in the World Skate Cross Series and since moving to Seattle, has competed in roller derby as a member of the Rat City Rollergirls.

Naomi is a qualified Level 3 instructor under the IISA Instructor Certification Programme, and is the sole trainer and certifier of ICP and SkateIA freestyle slalom instructors worldwide. She has conducted over 100 of her highly successful weekend and week-long freestyle slalom courses held in Europe, Asia, the USA and Australia, with many participants going on to represent their nations in international competition.

Acknowledgements

Berti Dempster for taking this skater who was unable to reach beyond 'do it like this … no … like this' and turn her into a successful instructor.

Asha Kirkby and Jonathan Acott for taking me into their skate school and showing me the ropes of teaching as a business, particularly Asha for always being someone whose teaching quality I still strive to match.

Sebastien Laffargue for being a role model in the arena of working hard and unwaveringly for the good of skating, and time and time again demonstrating what it is to put skating and skaters above one's own gain. If it wasn't for the hard work and dedication to whatever he is creating that Sebastien shows on a continual basis, then I would have held myself to much lower standards over the years and this book certainly would never have materialised.

My mother, Pamela Clark, for the multiple proof-readings of this book and 'patiently forcing' me to endure the process of working through the hundreds of editing changes and corrections, one by painful one, over a series of days that must have strained her far more than she ever let on.

Last but definitely not least, I would like to acknowledge my publisher, David Harrison, for going far beyond the role of publisher in order to bring this book to publication.

Author's Note

I would like to thank my publisher, David Harrison, who has not only undertaken the challenge of the full publishing process, but has had to do so while I have pulled very, very hard in the opposite direction for fear that my words might end up on a precarious pedestal.

I had always loved the idea of getting this book published, but the closer I became to making it happen, the more lethargic and unmotivated I felt towards the project and would stop at an early hurdle. David had read my transcript online and wrote suggesting that perhaps he could help, which I expected would take the form of his assisting me while I took the lead.

How very wrong I was, for very shortly afterwards, version 1 of *The Art of Falling* arrived unannounced and unexpectedly in my mailbox, revealing the countless hours of undisclosed effort that David had already invested.

Once I realised that he was taking the lead, David's uphill struggle of dragging me along the journey began in earnest, for he didn't just do all of the work to get the book to your hands, he also had to ensure that I stepped up to the author's role in the process. I want to acknowledge David for patiently managing me throughout this process and doing so without any detectable judgement or frustration while enduring phases of having his emails ignored for lengthy periods, my unwillingness to write extra sections that were needed, my avoidance of any proof-reading or decision making … and I am sure the list goes on.

David has toiled over this book, edited it, funded it, suggested content alterations, and provided a vision for what the finished product could become.

In the end, this book is a true example of a team effort. It could not exist without the equal efforts of both the author and this particular publisher, for I'm absolutely sure that no other publisher would have matched the time and effort that it took to write it in order to push this project through to its eventual publication.

Naomi Grigg

Printed in Great Britain
by Amazon